Aloha!

Chieko N. Okazaki

Deseret Book Company
Salt Lake City, Utah

Library of Congress Cataloging-in-Publication Data

Okazaki, Chieko N., 1926–
    Aloha! / Chieko N. Okazaki.
       p.   cm.
    Includes bibliographical references.
    ISBN 0-87579-979-5
    1. Christian life—Mormon authors. I. Title.
BX8656.O43   1995
248.4'89332—dc20

                                       94-45860
                                          CIP

Printed in the United States of America
10 9 8 7 6 5 4 3 2 1

To my mother,
Hatsuko Nishi Nishimura

Contents

PART 1

Circles of Sisterhood

CHAPTER 1

Strength from the Savior

The Church teaches us all the principles and doctrine that make it possible to create an ideal family: a mother and father sealed in the temple and sealed by the Holy Spirit of Promise in love for each other and for the children who come to their home. In this family, the parents and children support, sustain, and love one another, seek the Lord through prayer and scripture study, both individually and together, set high goals, and work together to achieve them. They reach out to extended family members and to neighbors. They are confident in the gospel, humble in their strength to resist temptation, joyful in their testimony of the Savior's atonement. In such circumstances, the ideal of a Christ-centered family seems happily attainable.

But, President Ezra Taft Benson pointed out, only 14 percent of American households in 1980 matched the traditional image of a couple with children still in the home. (See "Fundamentals of Enduring Family Relationships," *Ensign*, Nov. 1982, p. 59.) According to reliable sources, only one in five Latter-day Saint families in the United States has a husband and wife married in the temple with children in their home. The comparable figure for Saints in Japan is one in thirty-three. (See Tim B. Heaton, "Vital Statistics: Demographic

3

Characteristics," *Encyclopedia of Mormonism,* ed. Daniel H. Ludlow [New York: Macmillan, 1992], 4:1532.)

If I were to ask you what the Church teaches about strengthening families, I know that you would say things like, "spend time together, have family prayer, hold family home evening, and have regular scripture study." In addition to these important things, I want to talk about building stronger families by building a stronger you—strong in your faith in the Savior. *That's* where strong families come from—from strong individuals.

President Gordon B. Hinckley has said: "The strength of the Church is not in its thousands of houses of worship across the world nor in its universities or seminaries and institutes. These are all facilities, desirable means to an end, but only auxiliary to that which is the true strength. The strength of this Church lies in the hearts of its people, in the individual testimony and conviction of the truth of this work." ("'It's True, Isn't It?'" *Ensign,* July 1993, p. 4.)

Just as the Church's strength lies in the individual members, so the strength of each family lies in its members. There is great diversity in LDS homes, but all of these homes can be righteous homes in which individuals love each other, love the Lord, and strengthen each other.

Let me give you an example. Consider two quilts. Both are handmade, beautiful, and delightful to snuggle down in or wrap around a grandchild. One quilt is a Hawaiian quilt with a strong, predictable pattern. We can look at half of the quilt and predict what the other half will look like. Sometimes our lives seem patterned, predictable in happy ways, in order.

Imagine a second quilt. Its style is called a crazy quilt.

Some pieces are the same color, but no two pieces are the same size. They're odd shapes. They come together at odd angles. This is an unpredictable quilt. Sometimes our lives are unpredictable, unpatterned, not neat or well ordered.

Well, there's not one right way to be a quilt as long as the pieces are stitched together firmly. Both of these quilts will keep us warm and cozy. Both are beautiful and made with love. There's not just one right way to be a Mormon woman, either, as long as we are firmly grounded in faith in the Savior, make and keep covenants, live the commandments, and work together in charity.

All of us face different family circumstances and home situations. All of us need strength in dealing with them. The Spirit of Christ is not a luxury to be enjoyed only when we have achieved an ideal environment. It is the essential transforming power that can lift and strengthen us amid the trials of real life, even when our situations are far from perfect.

It is possible, even in less than ideal circumstances, to have a Christ-centered home. The process of building a Christ-centered home can begin with a single faithful individual: ourselves. We do not have to wait to have a Christ-centered home until we have achieved perfect faith, any more than we have to have perfect circumstances first. We just need growing faith and a desire to work toward the ideal. According to Doctrine and Covenants 46, gifts are given to all. We are people in process, and that process is coming about as we keep the commandments of God and learn the doctrine of the Church.

What kind of strength do we need as women? We need the Savior's strength. It comes from faith in the Savior's love and in the power of his atonement. If we trustingly put our hand in the Savior's, we can claim the promise of our baptism to always have his Spirit with us. All problems are manageable with that strength, and all problems are secondary in urgency to maintaining a strong spiritual life.

If we have faith, we will desire to pray often and sincerely, and his Spirit will teach us what to pray for. (See Romans 8:26–27.) We will have the sensitivity to serve compassionately in our neighborhood. We will have the wisdom that we need for our church callings. We can build loving and respectful partnerships with our husband, children, parents, and friends. If we always have Christ's Spirit with us, we will have a wise consultant when we are perplexed by our children's needs. We will receive help in making correct decisions and strength in carrying them out. We will give and receive loyal friendship and feel in ourselves when the advice we receive from others is truly suited to our needs. We will hold a clear vision of gospel ideals and aspire toward them even as we deal patiently with the limitations of reality. Through faith in the Savior we can magnify our opportunities, cope with our problems, and keep both of them in perspective.

One precious account of a righteous couple rearing faithful children is the story of Jairus and his wife. The father sought out Jesus when their beloved twelve-year-old daughter was on the point of death. "Fear not," Jesus told him when messengers intercepted Him on the way with news that the child had died. "Believe only, and she shall be made whole." (Luke 8:50.) Mother and father together witnessed the fruit of their faith as their daughter was restored to them. Sorrow was averted by a miracle, thanks to their faith.

But even faithful couples cannot guarantee the salvation

of all their children. Adam and Eve were certainly magnificent in their faith, but one of their sons was a murderer. Lehi and Sariah sacrificed their all in obedience to the Lord's commandment, but their disobedient sons racked the family with strife and conflict.

And many families must deal with circumstances in which there is no spouse to provide support and comfort through times of trial. Think of the widow of Nain as she walked behind the bier of her only son, the child who would have been both the economic and the emotional mainstay of her old age. She was already a single mother, earlier visited by the sorrow of losing her husband. We can guess something of her despair, but we know nothing of her faith. The scriptural record does not say that she appealed to Jesus for help; rather, Jesus saw her tears, "had compassion on her, and said unto her, Weep not." She may not even have understood what was happening when Jesus stopped the procession and raised her son from the dead. But all of us can imagine the faith and gratitude that bloomed like sudden flowers in that widow's heart as her living son was restored to her. (See Luke 7:11–15.)

Think of Mary, Martha, and Lazarus. The scriptures refer to the home as Martha's. (See Luke 10:38.) Mary and Lazarus may have lived with her. The scriptures do not mention that any of them were married. Even though their family had a less than ideal configuration, Jesus did not find them unworthy of his love and attention. Gladly Jesus came to their home, and joyfully he taught them his gospel. When Lazarus died, Jesus shared the sisters' grief even as he called Lazarus forth from the grave. (See John 11:1–44.)

Think of the mother of James and John. Certainly she had

faith, for the scriptures tell us that she "worship[ped]" Jesus and begged him to guarantee a sure place in heaven for her sons, one at Jesus' right hand and the other at his left. (See Matthew 20:20–21.) What mother would not desire to guarantee her children's salvation? But the Savior explained why even this apparently righteous request could not be granted. Surely her faith had room to grow into a fuller understanding that her sons were being called, not to a guarantee of glory, but to a life of service. "Whosoever will be great among you," reminded Jesus, "let him be your minister; And whosoever will be chief among you, let him be your servant." (Matthew 20:26–27.) Salvation is not a prize to be hoarded within even the most loving family but the natural product of a life of service.

Think of the Samaritan woman at the well, married five times and then living with a man not her husband. Certainly those were not ideal circumstances in which to raise children, nor had her faith been sufficient to give her a more peaceful, less turbulent lifestyle. Surely she was a strange candidate for revelation, but Jesus looked past her circumstances, past her current level of faith to her potential, and she became the first person to whom he revealed that he was the son of God, the Messiah. She ran back to her town, sharing her newfound testimony. (See John 4:1–26.)

Think of Abraham and Sarah, dealing with the sorrow of infertility for so many years of their married life. Think of Esther's far from ideal circumstances—married to a man who was not only an unbeliever but a pagan, and isolated from her uncle and fellow believers. Still, her faith was sufficient to make her the instrument of salvation to her people.

What is the message of those stories? First, we do not need

to wait for ideal circumstances before Jesus can enter our lives. Jesus came to save people who were not perfect, to heal people who were not already healthy, to show a better way to people who had gone astray. He will enter our homes, too, even though they are not perfect, if we open our doors to him. "Behold," he has said, "I stand at the door, and knock." (Revelation 3:20.) Sometimes we think we cannot live the principles of the gospel because we are not in ideal circumstances. We need to stretch toward Christ, and in so doing we will find that our capacity increases.

We do not need to wait for perfect faith to have enough faith to begin building Christ-centered families. When the apostles could not cast an evil spirit out of a boy, the father carried him to Jesus, who gave him a piercing challenge: "If thou canst believe, all things are possible." The father, knowing the imperfect state of his faith but also his desire for more, cried out, weeping, "Lord, I believe; help thou mine unbelief." (Mark 9:23–24.) Jesus did not rebuke him or say, "Come back when you have more faith." He healed the child.

The scriptures show us examples of families with whom Jesus interacted during his premortal and mortal ministries. They had hearts willing to receive him even if their circumstances were not ideal. They had faith and yearned for more. They sacrificed, served others, prayed, fasted, and pondered the promises of the prophets.

What is our Heavenly Father's work and glory? It is "to bring to pass [our] immortality and eternal life." (Moses 1:39.) The work of salvation goes on *despite* imperfect circumstances and imperfect faith. "I am come that they might have life," the Savior explained, "and that they might have it more

9

abundantly." (John 10:10.) His task was not only to give life to the dead, miraculous though that was, but to give increased life to those living with less than flourishing faith, less than vibrant hope, less than burning charity.

He accepts our imperfections even as he challenges us to rise above them. He loves us even when we are not very lovable. He rewards even a struggling faith with miracles.

Because we understand the doctrine of the ideal family, we can be grateful for the parts of it that we possess. We are grateful for the guidance that comes to us from prophets, apostles, and other Church leaders. We can strengthen our family's relationship with Christ by faith, hope, and charity: *faith* that our prayers will be answered and that our testimonies can be shared; *hope* that persistent service, good example, and true teachings will eventually prevail; and *charity* that creates love and acceptance within our homes.

Strong families build strong individuals who, in turn, are able to strengthen other family members. We take turns in lifting each other. I have seen this process at work in my own life.

When my husband and I married, I was a Latter-day Saint and he was a Congregationalist. We both shared a strong faith in the Savior, and I felt that someone as honest and loving as Ed would continue to seek and accept truth. I shared my testimony with Ed, and ten months after our marriage, he was baptized. We were the only Latter-day Saints in our families, but we could strengthen each other.

When Ed was ordained to the Melchizedek Priesthood, the concept of priesthood was a thrilling and exciting one for us. He was the first priesthood holder in the Okazaki family, and I, of course, had no relatives who were priesthood holders. It was

10

something we talked about and worked to understand together. How grateful I was for Ed's goodness, his Christlike desire to serve others, and the many opportunities that the Church gave him to exercise his priesthood on behalf of us, our sons, and others. There were many tender moments as he gave father's blessings to our two sons—not only when they were ill but when they needed comfort and strength, or to mark special events like school years, new church responsibilities, and their missions. Ed never took his priesthood for granted. It was always a privilege to him, one exercised with thanksgiving and humility. Supporting Ed in his callings and feeling his support for me in mine was part of the partnership of our marriage.

After we moved back to Salt Lake City in 1988, we were invited to an interview with the Missionary Committee. We suspected that a calling might be in the offing, so Ed, who had had a stroke about two years earlier that affected his heart, went to the doctor first so that he would know if he could accept an assignment. The doctor was absolutely firm that Ed must not leave the country. Thus, when the Missionary Committee discussed the possibility of Ed's being called to preside over a Missionary Training Center in another country, Ed was very disappointed to have to tell them the doctor's instructions. I would have supported Ed wholeheartedly in his calling, but it was not to be.

Then, a few weeks later, I was called to serve on the Primary General Board, and a year and a half later, I was called to be first counselor in the Relief Society general presidency. When I was being set apart, President Thomas S. Monson, who had known us for years, said, "Eddie, Chieko has supported you in your priesthood callings—in the bishopric, as mission president, and as regional representative. Now it's your turn to support her." Ed smiled and agreed to do so. What President Monson may not have known is that was not a change for Ed.

Ed and I loved teaching our sons the gospel and a strong faith in the Savior. We were grateful we had the strength to care for them and grateful to see them grow up to become independent and self-reliant people with the strength to help others. We rejoiced in the strength that an intelligent and sensitive daughter-in-law brought to our family. We delighted in seeing our grandsons born and begin to follow the cycle of family life themselves.

I never appreciated the strength of my sons more than when my husband was dying. All three of us sustained each other and consulted with each other, but Ken took the lead in working with the doctors and the hospital. Then when Ed died, Bob took the lead in making funeral arrangements and dealing with the legal procedures that had to be followed. In planning the funeral service, I took the lead. As each of us passed through different stages in our shock and grief, we had the others for support. When one of us needed to rise to an occasion, we could. When we needed to withdraw with our sorrow, we could because one of the others could step forward and be the leader.

I have used the example of my own family, because I have seen for myself that it is to our family that we turn in such crises. Yet whatever our family or marital circumstances, the strength we need can always be found because it comes from the Savior and his love. Sometimes our own faith enables us to draw on that love. Sometimes it is the faith and love of others that strengthens us.

12

We do not know the challenges and adversities that life will give us. But the scriptures promise us that "with God nothing shall be impossible" (Luke 1:37), and we can say with the apostle Paul, "I can do all things through Christ which strengtheneth me" (Philippians 4:13).

The scriptures are filled with testimonies of the strength that comes from the Savior. I particularly love the encouragement and lift of the heart that comes to me when I read these rejoicings of the prophets:

Moses exulted, "The Lord is my strength and song, and he is become my salvation." (Exodus 15:2.)

David sang, "God is my strength and power: and he maketh my way perfect." (2 Samuel 22:33.)

The psalmist testified, "God is our refuge and strength, a very present help in trouble. Therefore [we] will not . . . fear, though the earth be removed, and though the mountains be carried into the midst of the sea." (Psalm 46:1–2.)

To Isaiah, the Lord promised: "Fear thou not; for I am with thee: be not dismayed; for I am thy God: I will strengthen thee; yea, I will help thee; yea, I will uphold thee with the right hand of my righteousness." (Isaiah 41:10.)

How can we build that kind of faith in the strength of the Savior? David had counsel for the people of his time that I repeat to you: "Seek the Lord and his strength, seek his face continually. Remember his marvellous works that he hath done, his wonders, and the judgments of his mouth." (1 Chronicles 16:11–12.) "Blessed is the man [or woman] whose strength is in thee; in whose heart are [thy] ways. . . . Go from strength to strength." (Psalm 84:5, 7.)

Strengthen yourselves by seeking the source of true

strength: the Savior. Come unto him. He loves you. He desires your happiness and exults in your desires for righteousness. Make him your strength, your daily companion, your rod and your staff. Let him comfort you. There is no burden we need bear alone. We do not need to wait for perfect faith to have *enough* faith. He meets our need. His grace compensates for our deficiencies. He is willing and eager, if we will only ask.

Your strength will strengthen others—your children, your husband, your friends, and your sisters in the gospel. That strength will flow back from them to you when you need it.

Through the years, the circumstances of my life have changed. I was a single woman, then a wife married to a non-member, then a partner in a temple sealing, a mother, a mother-in-law and grandmother, and now a widow. I have known the Savior's love in all of these circumstances. My own faith has been rewarded as I have felt the Savior's presence and power in my home.

Our circumstances will not always be ideal, but we can still strive to live up to our ideals, to strengthen our faith, and to do the best we can. We can draw on the Savior's power to strengthen us as individuals and families. From the bottom of my heart and from more than fifty years of experience in the Church, I testify that the Savior extends to us all the same mercy, the same power to find healing, and the same perfect love. He has assured us that it is his work and glory to bring to pass our immortality and eternal life. What joy it gives us to contemplate eternal life with our families as part of the great family of God. What warmth and what beauty come from every well-made quilt, even crazy quilts.

CHAPTER 2

Sisterhood and Service

The gospel teaches us the joy of service. It teaches us about Jesus Christ, whose whole life was one of service. And it teaches us how to serve.

After a year of thinking about service during 1992 as part of the sesquicentennial of the Relief Society, all of us have broadened and deepened our understanding. In connection with that principle, let me share with you a legend from my homeland of Hawaii. It is significant to me that many of the powers we Christians associate with the Savior were the province of goddesses in the ancient tales and legends of Hawaii. This legend from the big island of Hawaii is a story of divine sacrifice that has, I think, some parallels with the sacrifice of the Savior, though expressed in ways that the ancient Hawaiians could understand.

You may know that the island of Maui, according to the legends of Hawaii, was named for the son of the goddess Hina. It is not so well known that Hina also had four daughters. Near the city of Hilo, on the big island, are three small craters that are particularly associated with one of those daughters, Hina Keahi, whose name signifies her control of fire. According to the legend of the place, the mother Hina gave Hina Keahi the area near Hilo where she ruled over her

15

people and her children. For a long time they lived in peace and prosperity. The land was fertile, and the rains came often.

But at last the days were like fire and the sky had no rain in it. The taro planted on the hillsides died. The bananas and sugar cane and sweet potatoes withered and the fruit on the trees was blasted. The people were faint because of hunger, and the shadow of death was over the land.

Hina Keahi pitied her suffering friends and determined to provide food for them. Slowly her people labored at her command, . . . gathering and carrying back whatever wood they could find, then went up the mountainside to the great koa and ohia forests, gathering their burdens of fuel according to the wishes of the [goddess].

. . . After many days the great quantity of wood desired by the goddess was piled up by the side of the Halai Hill.

Then came the days of digging out the hill and making a great imu or cooking oven, and preparing it with stones and wood. Large quantities of wood were thrown into the place. Stones best fitted for retaining heat were gathered and the fires kindled. When the stones were hot, Hina Keahi directed the people to arrange the imu in its proper order for cooking . . . a great feast. A place was made for sweet potatoes, another for taro, another for pigs, and another for dogs. All the forms of preparing the food for cooking were passed through, but no real food was laid on the stones.

Then Hina Keahi told them to make a place in the imu for a human sacrifice. . . . Therefore it was in quiet despair that the workmen obeyed Hina Keahi. . . . It might mean their own holocaust as an offering to the gods. At last Hina Keahi bade the laborers . . . [to] stand by the side of the oven, ready to cover it with the dirt which had been thrown up and piled up by the side. The people stood by, not knowing upon whom the blow might fall.

But [although] Hina Keahi . . . stood before them robed in

16

royal majesty and power, still her face was full of pity and love. Her voice melted the hearts of her retainers as she bade them carefully follow her directions:

"O my people! . . . This imu is my imu. I shall lie down in its bed of burning stones. . . . I shall sleep under its cover. . . . Quickly throw the dirt over my body. Fear not the fire." . . .

Hina Keahi was very beautiful and her eyes flashed light like fire as she stepped into the great pit and lay down on the burning stones. A great smoke arose and gathered over the imu. The men toiled rapidly, placing the imu mats over [her] and throwing the dirt back into the oven until it was all thoroughly covered and the smoke was quenched. . . . The great heat of the fire in the imu withered the little life that was still left [in the surrounding countryside] from the famine.

Meanwhile Hina Keahi was carrying out her plan for . . . her people. [Although her people were sure that she was dying, smothered by the smoke and burned by the flames] she could not be injured by the heat, for she was a goddess of fire. The waves of heat raged around her as she sank down through the stones of the imu into the underground paths which belonged to the spirit world.

On the first day, there burst forth a gushing stream of water. On the second day, closer to the sea, appeared a pool of water. And on the third day, on the beach "in the very path of the ocean surf burst forth a great spring of sweet water." A beautiful woman appeared at the imu and commanded the starving people to dig away the dirt and pull back the mats. "When this was done, the hungry people found a very great abundance of food, enough to supply their wants until the food plants should have time to ripen and the days of the famine should be over. The joy of the people was great." (W. D. Westervelt, *Myths and Legends of Hawaii,* sel. A. Grove

Day [Honolulu: Mutual Publishing/Tales of the Pacific, 1987], pp. 25–29.)

I love thinking about this legend of Hina Keahi, who saw suffering and had compassion on the sufferers and who was willing to sacrifice herself for her people out of the love and generosity of her heart. This story embodies the belief of the Hawaiian people that love, generosity, and sacrifice in behalf of others can make great miracles. If you have experienced the aloha spirit of Hawaii, you know that those same principles still make Hawaii the special place that it is. But love and generosity are miracles wherever they occur. The service that takes place within a network of sisters is one of the most beautiful manifestations of charity, or the divine love of Christ, that we can experience in mortality. Each kindly deed weaves another strand in the gospel pattern of love and service.

I want to discuss sisterhood and service in three of its many aspects. First, let me share with you some of the amazing things that happen when sisters work together in groups. Second, let me suggest some of the even more amazing things that can happen when we have the will within ourselves to act on our own in offering individual service. And third, let me share my testimony about the power available when men and women work together in harmony.

WORKING TOGETHER

Following is just a sampling of some of the joyful reports we have received from Relief Society sisters all over the world who have found a way to reach out to their communities during the sesquicentennial year. Many of these projects have

18

been in the self-sacrificial spirit of Hina Keahi, responding with compassion to the needs of the people around them.

In South Africa, the Benoni Ward is visiting and serving at a home for old-age pensioners.

In Australia's Gosford Ward, sisters are working to establish a youth detoxification center.

In France, the Versailles Ward is sending packages and letters to Romanian families whose immigrant brothers live in the ward.

The tiny Covington Branch Relief Society in Georgia was organized only recently, in February 1991, but every active member was present at the first homemaking meeting, and they chose to adopt a highway for cleaning.

The Ashford Ward of Rhode Island Stake is providing service at a camp for children with cancer.

The Staten Island Ward in New York wrapped Christmas packages at a mall to earn money for material for quilts to give to shelters for abused women and children.

Southington First Ward in Connecticut is coordinating a soup kitchen with the local council of churches.

In Yugoslavia, sisters in Zagreb are aiding refugees from the war.

Sisters in a ward at Brigham Young University made flash cards for Vietnamese refugees to help them learn English.

In Orem, Utah, one group of sisters makes teddy bears to be carried in police cars to comfort little children in need.

A group of sisters in Tennessee helps adults who are trying to pass their high school equivalency examinations.

In Santa Monica Second Ward in California, sisters made protective cases for magnifying lenses and gave them to a local institute that serves the partially sighted. (See Sheridan R. Sheffield, "Celebrate through Service," *Church News,* 25 Apr. 1992.)

In Micronesia, on the small island of Ebeye, where there are about three hundred Church members among a population of thirteen thousand, the Relief Society sisters have spent time picking up litter every Wednesday. After the first few times, the queen of the island joined them. (Ibid.)

A presesquicentennial project in the Huntington Beach Fourth Ward did great things with small resources but enormous love for the women and children in an emergency shelter. Early in 1990, the Relief Society presidency asked the sisters to look through their sewing boxes and donate fabric they weren't using or scraps left over from a project. They also asked for yarn and batting. Judy Lockhart, the Relief Society president, wrote:

> The response was overwhelming! We sorted the fabric into heaps by colors—every color of the rainbow was there—and miraculously there was a skein of yarn just the right color to go with each heap of fabric.
>
> The sisters took the fabric home and each worked individually on making one or more pieced quilts from the fabric they had. They constructed a quilt top as well as a back. Some sisters made one; some made eight or ten. The Merrie Miss class made a complete quilt, tied it, and finished the edges.

In one twelve-hour marathon that included the Young Women during the evening, these sisters tied forty-one quilts, ranging from baby- or youth-size to twins and doubles. Sister Lockhart summarized, "The spirit of the event was indescribable. We learned skills, we were able to give generously of our time and talents, we were able to socialize as we worked."

And they provided gifts of warmth and love to many women who must have felt that the world was a dangerous and uncaring place.

This same Relief Society has taken on the therapy of a young man who had been paralyzed in a car accident and who was slowly dying in bed for lack of the ability to pay for the intensive therapy he needed. These generous-hearted sisters have involved their husbands and even their teenage children in this young man's therapy. After talking with his parents, Sister Lockhart says, "I was humbled to know that we are the answer to their prayers." (Letter to Relief Society General Presidency, 12 Nov. 1991.)

We are literally answers to prayers when we are willing to serve. It is a lovely thought that, all around the world, these acts of kindly service are occurring, linking sister to sister, Relief Society to Relief Society, and human being to human being. They are part of the loving and sacrificial spirit of the legend of Hina Keahi.

Sometimes we get discouraged because the needs in the world around us seem so great and our resources seem so few. We think, "We're not doing enough. We can't do enough. Nobody could do enough." When we think like that, we focus on what is left undone, and we lose the joy that comes with service. I want to tell you that we don't need to compare ourselves to anyone else, either collectively or as individuals. Lighten up. Concentrate on the joy, not the job. We can do great good when we work as a united sisterhood, as long as we don't burden ourselves with unrealistic expectations that rob us of the joy of achievement.

SERVICE AS INDIVIDUALS

Another side of service is our ability to do good as individuals. Just a single individual can set amazing things in motion if he or she has the sensitivity to see a human need and has the will to respond to it. It takes special eyes to see that we are not just individual strands but rather that we are all part of the cat's cradle of caring. President Gordon B. Hinckley, expressing the credo that has shaped his life, bore a powerful testimony about the importance of individual service:

> Though my work may be menial, though my contribution may be small, I can perform it with dignity and offer it with unselfishness. My talents may not be great, but I can use them to bless the lives of others. I can be one who does his work with pride in that which comes from hand and mind. I can be one who works with respect for my associates, for their opinions, for their beliefs, with appreciation for their problems and with a desire to help them should they stumble. I believe in the principle that I can make a difference in this world. It may be ever so small. But it will count for the greater good. The goodness of the world in which we live is the accumulated goodness of many small and seemingly inconsequential acts. ("I Believe," *Ensign,* Aug. 1992, p. 7)

President Hinckley has the quality of *kigatsuku.* This important Japanese concept, which I learned from my mother when I was a very small child, means an inner spirit to see good and do it, without being told and without being organized into a service project. My husband, Ed, was *kigatsuku* his entire life, always thinking ahead in his assignments. He liked the story of Hina Keahi because of the goddess's gentle and loving spirit. When he was executive secretary in the Littleton

22

Colorado Stake presidency, he would go early for the stake presidency and high council meetings, arrange the chairs, sharpen the pencils, and lay out copies of the agenda. During the meeting, he would make notes about upcoming events and quietly see that the stake president had reminders when he needed them. Nobody told him that was part of his job when he was called. And Ed wasn't the kind to go around only reading books and manuals on how to be the perfect executive secretary—although I think he came pretty close to achieving it. He did what he did because his heart was in the right place. He was constantly asking himself, "How can I help the stake president and the high councilors? What can I do to make their work easier? What needs do I see, and what can I do about them?" Second-mile service for him was second nature.

Here's a wonderful story about doing just what you can. A deputy answered a call to the Knox County, Tennessee, sheriff's department about a woman crying uncontrollably in a restaurant. Two girls, perhaps four and five years old, anxiously watched their mother. " 'Daddy left us,' [one] blurted. 'He just put our stuff out of the car while we was in the bathroom.' "

The officer sent the little girls to the counter to order something to eat, and he signaled the waitress to take their order. Then he asked the woman what the problem was. " 'Just what my girl said,' she replied, wiping her eyes with the back of her hand. 'My husband's not cruel—just at the end of his rope. We're flat broke, and he figured we'd get more help alone than if he stayed.' "

Her nearest family was in Chicago, so they talked about local agencies that could help. When the waitress took hot dogs and french fries to the little girls, the officer went to the counter to pay.

"'The boss says no charge,' the waitress said. 'We know what's going on.'

"'Officer, excuse me.' A big man in jeans, T-shirt, and baseball cap stood by the counter." The other patrons in the restaurant watched without speaking.

"'Here,' he said, extending a handful of bills. 'We passed the hat. . . . Tell her it was from folks with families of their own.'"

There was enough money for the woman and her daughters to buy bus tickets to Chicago and meals during their journey. When the deputy put the money into the woman's hand, she began to cry again. (See David Hunter, "Truck-Stop Samaritans," in "Heroes for Today," *Reader's Digest,* Jan. 1992, pp. 142–43.)

What I love about this story is that many people became part of the solution to the woman's problem. But did you notice what the officer *didn't* say? Not one of the people there had made a move to help the woman before he got there. Someone had telephoned the police to say, "There's this woman who won't stop crying and she has two little girls with her," but everyone waited for someone else to do something first. Perhaps because he had an official position, the officer was the key to the solution, but what exactly did he do? He sat down and asked her one question. And he was willing to pay for the girls' hot dogs—but he didn't even have to do that. As soon as it became apparent that the girls were hungry, someone else took care of providing for that need. That's *kigatsuku* service—reaching out to do what you can, even if you're not sure that you can solve the problem, even if you're not sure that anyone else will help, and even if you're not sure that there are enough resources of the right kind to solve the problem. In more cases than you'd think, a cat's cradle of caring will spring up. Even though the truck drivers and the waitresses didn't feel as individuals that they could solve the problem, they were all willing to help become part of the solution when they could see a pattern start to form.

And here's an equally inspiring story about one Latter-day Saint woman, Vicki Vehar, who made a great difference because she took seriously the Book of Mormon scripture, "When ye are in the service of your fellow beings ye are only in the service of your God." (Mosiah 2:17.) Vicki, a member of Naperville Second Ward in Chicago, was greatly struck by that scripture when she was investigating the Church. She has always taken time for community service, even though she is very busy as a financial planner, wife, mother, and now worker in the Chicago Temple.

> When she read about a program in which excess food [was] collected from places such as restaurants and grocery stores and distributed to food banks and shelters for the homeless, she believed it was an idea that could work in her area. She began investigating the availability of surplus food and the need for it in the Chicago area. One of the places she called to offer help in arranging for food was the Salvation Army.
>
> The night following her call, a freak tornado struck the Plainsfield-Joliet area, about thirty-five miles southwest of Chicago. The twister plowed down a three-mile swath several blocks wide, destroying everything in its path and killing twelve people. The next morning, Vicki received a call from the same Salvation Army worker she had spoken

to the previous day: Could she possibly help provide some volunteers to assist the tornado victims?

Although this wasn't the kind of help she had originally offered, it was still an opportunity to serve. Vicki called the mission president, and within an hour, eight missionaries—one couple, four elders, and two sisters—were on the scene. The women distributed hamburgers and other foodstuffs, donated by a national fast-food chain, to people whose homes had been destroyed; the men began helping with the salvage process.

The next morning, Vicki got an elated phone call from the woman at the Salvation Army. "I don't know how you did it, but your church is absolutely wonderful!" the woman exclaimed. (Derin Head Rodriguez, "Reaching Out," *Ensign,* Jan. 1992, p. 70)

Vicki is a *kigatsuku* woman, busily and beautifully involved in a cat's cradle of caring.

Let's not be afraid to take the first step when we see a need and to do what we can, even if it looks as if it couldn't possibly be enough or be really helpful.

BUILDING THE KINGDOM

The third concept about service that I want to share with you involves men and women working together in harmony in mutually supportive relationships that recognize and honor the differences and similarities between men and women, that draw deeply on the strengths of both, that focus on working toward righteous goals, and that celebrate the contributions of both in the home, in the community, and in the church and kingdom of God. I was very touched when President Howard W. Hunter spoke in the general women's meeting in September 1992. I love President Hunter, the gentleness and the clarity of his manner, and the obvious love he has for all members of the Church. He said: "By reason of our call to testify, govern, and minister, it is required of us that despite age, infirmity, exhaustion, and feelings of inadequacy, we do the work he has given us to do, to the last breath of our lives. As our Lord and Savior needed the women of his time . . . —even in his hour of humiliation, agony, and death—so we, his servants, all across the Church, need you, the women of the Church, to stand with us and for us." ("To the Women of the Church," *Ensign,* Nov. 1992, p. 96.)

I, with you, felt within myself the desire to respond even more strongly to that call from a priesthood leader. Sometimes the opportunity to stand with and for our priesthood leaders comes about in ways we may not expect or understand. Let me tell you of an experience I had not long ago.

I was assigned to speak at a regional Relief Society meeting. Before I went, I conferred with the host stake Relief Society president and the host stake president about the needs of the sisters in that area and felt deeply impressed to address directly one of the items on their list: sexual abuse. I had many misgivings about speaking on this subject. I am far from being an expert on it. I had great feelings of inadequacy. Yet I knew in my soul that I was receiving promptings to do so. I prayed with humility for assistance. Afterward I discovered that the need was indeed a serious one and that many women and priesthood leaders in the audience had been praying for that message and so were already prepared to hear it. One was a bishop who came up to speak with me afterwards. His eyes filled with tears as he told me about being prompted strongly and repeatedly to address the topic of sexual abuse with his

27

ward members. Bishops who have dealt with this subject sensitively have been able to help those who have suffered the indignity and the pain of abuse.

I have spoken here of abuse not only because it is an example that is fresh in my mind on account of my recent experiences but because all of us can understand how important it is for the survivors of childhood sexual abuse, particularly incest, to see examples of men and women working together in healthy ways for the good of others.

As I think of the next one hundred fifty years of the Relief Society, I foresee the flowering of the great work that I believe Joseph Smith had in mind when he organized the women in Nauvoo. It is a great joy to support the priesthood, to see our different strengths, our different perspectives, and our different gifts unite in righteousness to be dedicated to the Lord. I see a greater acceptance of and rejoicing in the diversity among brothers and sisters in the kingdom, knowing that each person is important, no matter what the individual's circumstances may be. I see women acknowledging their own strength and that of their sisters and freely offering it in harmony with priesthood principles. I see the strength and the joy that come from being united in the great cause of building the kingdom.

I think of the partnership between my husband, Ed, and me. I have always shared everything in my life with Ed; and whether I have been excited, dismayed, upset, confused, or thrilled by something, Ed was always there to listen attentively, to ask clarifying questions, and to express his loving support. I still talk to Ed in my mind. We were married too long for that dialogue to stop. But it is hard to know that his steady eyes, his warm smile, and his own happy enthusiasm are no longer a living presence in my life.

Even though I would give anything to talk with him again and hear his answers, I know that I cannot expect any contact except as a rare and sweet occurrence. But one morning some months ago, I was lying in bed just before I needed to get up to go to an early meeting. I wasn't asleep. I was just relaxed. And I heard Ed call me, "Chick! Chick!" It was exactly what he used to do when he got out of the shower and I was still in bed. He wanted to be sure that I wouldn't oversleep and miss getting up on time. Oh, I jumped right up, calling, "Ed!" There was no answer, of course, but I felt so good!

Ever since he died, I've wondered where he is exactly, whether he knows what's happening with me and the boys, and I so desperately wanted just a little contact with him again. And so that was how he chose to come. I have to smile. It was so characteristic of Ed. That loving little service, that gentle support to help me with my calling, is exactly the service that Ed would have chosen to perform in life.

CONCLUSION

The support of my sisters in the Relief Society, not only on the general board but throughout the world, has been a great source of comfort to me. I have grown to appreciate anew the strength in our sisterhood.

The sesquicentennial year launched us into the next one hundred fifty years of service. The gospel will enter many new lands, and millions of women will hear its glad tidings. They will understand their eternal identity as daughters of God. Their hearts will be flooded with gratitude as they realize the opportunity mortality offers them to work out the promises made in the premortal existence and the beauties of eternal progress and eternal family life that await them in the post-mortal existence. The Relief Society will be a powerful part of their lives. It will reinforce the gospel principles that they learn from the missionaries and confirm all that is good in their own families and cultures. Relief Societies will truly be "nursing mothers" to their wards and branches, but more—Relief Societies will be "nursing mothers" to hundreds of communities as the women unite in righteous service, bringing health, happiness, and holiness where there has been pain, sorrow, and fear.

The Relief Society is a mighty sisterhood. There is a great force for good in our organized, group efforts to improve our communities and reach out to others in loving service. We have immense power in ourselves, through the Spirit, to see a need and to meet it quickly with the resources at hand. In so doing, I believe that we will seldom need to work alone but that co-workers and colleagues will be attracted to our cause. Remember the legend of Hina Keahi. Remember to lighten up, and to greet our opportunities for service with a light heart, instead of being burdened. Remember the cat's cradle and the networks of caring and service that we can build together. Remember the strength and power of women, daughters of Christ, united in the cause of building the kingdom of God on earth.

PART 2

Centered on Christ

CHAPTER 3

The Way, the Truth,
and the Life

"I am the way, the truth, and the life." (John 14:6.) Jesus
spoke those words in a very intimate gathering, during the
Passover supper that he ate with his apostles in the upper
room. It must have seemed like an island of peace before the
ocean of turmoil and pain that was rising outside. It would
end, just a few hours later, in the trial and crucifixion of Jesus.
Gently he prepared them for his departure, and lovingly he
comforted them with these words:

> Let not your heart be troubled: ye believe in God, believe
> also in me.
>
> In my Father's house are many mansions: if it were not
> so, I would have told you. I go to prepare a place for you.
>
> And if I go and prepare a place for you, I will come again,
> and receive you unto myself; that where I am, there ye may
> be also.
>
> And whither I go ye know, and the way ye know.
>
> Thomas saith unto him, Lord, we know not whither thou
> goest; and how can we know the way?
>
> Jesus saith unto him, I am the way, the truth, and the life:
> no [one] cometh unto the Father, but by me. (John 14:1–6)

Let's turn that statement into a question: Is Christ *our*

way? Is he *our* truth? Is he *our* life? If he is, we already have claimed the promise he gave us of untroubled hearts.

I'd like to discuss with you three implications of accepting Christ's way as our way. And I'd like to do it by using another metaphor of Christ—Christ as the cornerstone. First, I'd like to share some thoughts about what it means to make Christ our foundation, our cornerstone. Second, let's consider the role of kindness as part of a Christian life. And third, I'd like to talk about patience as essential in living a Christian life.

CHRIST THE CORNERSTONE

What does it mean to make Christ the cornerstone of our lives and to build on him as our foundation? You're all familiar with Paul's lovely description of the organization of the Church:

> Now therefore ye are no more strangers and foreigners, but fellowcitizens with the saints, and of the household of God;
> And are built upon the foundation of the apostles and prophets, Jesus Christ himself being the chief corner stone;
> In whom all the building fitly framed together groweth unto an holy temple in the Lord:
> In whom ye also are builded together for an habitation of God through the Spirit. (Ephesians 2:19–22)

To me, this scripture means that our feelings about ourselves and our relationships with others are founded upon and spring from Jesus Christ. If we accept him as our Savior, if we believe that he truly came to earth out of love for us to accomplish his atoning sacrifice and to redeem us from our selfishness and our shortsightedness and our sins, then it means that we are building for eternity and that nothing will be wasted. But if we have not made a commitment to Christ in our hearts and if we have not accepted his loving sacrifice on our behalf, then all of our achievements are bricks without mortar—solid and even beautiful in themselves but not connected to each other, not something that will help us discover our eternal identities and build lasting relationships in our families, in our friendships, and in our shared membership in this wonderful church.

I feel such gratitude for the sacramental promises of the Savior to always let his Spirit be with us. I feel such strength from his love for me. I feel such acceptance and compassion in how he deals with me day by day. I feel such a desire to follow him and to be the kind of person who is worthy of his name. In my prayers I feel the peace and comfort of that little circle of disciples around the Savior in the upper room, and it gives me strength to walk down the stairs and out the door in my own life into the demands, the adversities, and even the calamities and tragedies that daily life hands us. He has promised that he will be our never-failing companion. We can trust that promise.

I hope that all of us begin our day by spending some time with the Savior, feeling his Spirit and enjoying his love for us. I realize that there are many days when that time can be only a moment snatched very early, either before other obligations claim us or in a quiet crack between responsibilities. But it doesn't matter. Once we have learned to recognize the Savior, I think we realize that he is our companion, even as we fly through a list of demands, distractions, and duties. He is a help, an anchor.

I think that's what being the foundation means. It means

that there's a sure, safe place in our hearts that shapes all the rest of our lives. It doesn't matter how prettily we paint the walls or how attractively we arrange the furniture in a house where the foundation is cracked and unstable. It will all come down. But when the foundation is strong, we can attend to all of the painting, patching, and piano moving with confidence, knowing that the foundation is there.

I love Primary songs. I particularly enjoy the song "The Wise Man and the Foolish Man," which describes the parable of Jesus about the two house builders, one who built on a foundation of faith in God and the other who built on a sandy foundation. (See *Children's Songbook* [Salt Lake City: The Church of Jesus Christ of Latter-day Saints, 1989], p. 281.) Jesus is the rock on which we build our lives. Now, if we're all convinced about the importance of building our lives on our testimonies of the Savior, we're ready to talk about the second point, kindness.

KINDNESS

Have you ever noticed that the way of Christ takes us straight to other people? The purpose of a foundation is not to be the rest of the house. It's to provide the base for the house. In the household of the Saints that Paul talks about, Christ is the foundation and the cornerstone, but our work and our responsibilities lie among our brothers and sisters.

While I was thinking about this idea, I remembered an important scripture that also deals with a stone—this time, not the foundation stone that Christ represents but the stone in our relationships. You remember that when the Savior was teaching his disciples how to pray and why their Father in

Heaven felt so strongly about prayer that he commanded us to pray to him, he used the example of the fish and the stone. Let me read you these verses from Luke 11, adapted slightly to apply directly to us as women:

> And I say unto you, Ask, and it shall be given you; seek, and ye shall find; knock, and it shall be opened unto you.
>
> For every one that asketh receiveth; and [she] that seeketh findeth; and to [her] that knocketh it shall be opened.
>
> If a [daughter] shall ask bread of any of you that is a [mother], will [she] give [her] a stone? or if [she] ask a fish, will [she] for a fish give [her] a serpent?
>
> Or if [she] shall ask an egg, will [the mother] offer [her] a scorpion?
>
> If ye then, being evil, know how to give good gifts unto your children: how much more shall your heavenly Father give the Holy Spirit to them that ask him? (Luke 11:9–13)

You get the point. Our Heavenly Father is a loving parent. He is kind to us. He waits tenderly to give us good gifts, out of the bounty of his love for us. And we have learned to rely on that love. The challenge for us is to deal kindly with each other. We need to have the same sensitivity and tenderness toward those around us with needs. A sister might not ask us for an egg, but she may ask us to listen while she talks about how frightened she is as her mother slowly slips toward death. A daughter might not ask us for bread and fish, but she might ask for reassurance when friends seem scornful or for encouragement when she has a tough school assignment to do. Can we give support and empowerment and courage instead of doubts and fears?

We're not talking about anything complicated or difficult

here. We're talking about simple human kindness, ordinary courtesy, genuine warmth, attentive listening. These are things we can all do. I think of Mother Teresa and how simple and uncomplicated she makes the enormous task of helping the poor of Calcutta. I love to read about her life and study her words, because she's someone who really puts the gospel into action. Malcolm Muggeridge, a prize-winning journalist who did some documentaries of Mother Teresa for the BBC, describes her this way:

> Mother Teresa moved in [among the poor of Calcutta] and stayed. . . . She, a nun, rather slightly built, with a few rupees in her pocket; not particularly clever, or particularly gifted in the arts of persuasion. Just with this Christian love shining about her; in her heart and on her lips. Just prepared to follow her Lord, and in accordance with his instructions regard every derelict left to die in the streets as him; to hear in the cry of every abandoned child . . . the cry of the Bethlehem child. . . .
>
> To her they are all children of God, for whom Christ died, and so deserving of all love. If God counts the hairs of each of their heads, if none are excluded from the salvation the Crucifixion offers, who will . . . exclude them from earthly . . . esteem? . . . I never experienced so perfect a sense of human equality as with Mother Teresa among her poor. Her love for them, reflecting God's love, makes them equal, as brothers and sisters within a family are equal, however widely they differ in intellectual . . . attainments, in physical beauty and grace. (*Something Beautiful for God: Mother Teresa of Calcutta* [New York: Walker and Co./Phoenix Press, 1971; large print ed., 1984], pp. 10–12)

Sometimes we're hesitant to reach out to others because we're afraid. We're afraid that their needs are too great, that we won't know how to help effectively, or that we might be taken advantage of. I think it's possible that we may bungle things a few times when we're trying to help. We may give the wrong kind of service or give it at the wrong time. It's true that we may be taken advantage of. But if I have to make a mistake between being trusting and being suspicious, I'd rather be too trusting. If I have to make a choice between being too generous and too judging, I'd rather be too generous.

One Sunday the autumn before my husband died, we went to a sort of park under a viaduct on Salt Lake City's west side where every Sunday a woman has come to feed the homeless. Others have come to help, too, and that's what Ed was doing. He'd been at the store the day before, and he just picked up two crates of oranges, one for us and one that he drove down early on Sunday morning. We helped serve the plates until we had to leave for church, and as we were leaving, passing among the groups of men standing around or sitting on the grass, Ed saw a man, thin and unshaven, shivering in only a T-shirt. When I glanced back over my shoulder, there was my wonderful husband slipping off his jacket and helping this man into it. He just said quietly, "You need this more than I do," and then, in his shirt sleeves, he came walking toward me with the biggest smile on his face. Nothing in the world—and I mean nothing—made Ed as happy as helping someone else.

It can be the same for us. The Savior is not asking us to wipe out poverty or eradicate disease. He's just asking us to "give . . . unto one of these little ones a cup of cold water only in the name of a disciple," as he says in Matthew 10:42, to speak gently instead of harshly when our patience is tried, to pray for someone who makes a mistake rather than gossip about that someone, to smile and say hello instead of walking on by, to ask "How are you?" and then really listen to the answer. He's just asking us to do what we can in very little ways.

I remember being very touched when I read an article by Lois M. Collins, a Utah writer. She recalled seeing a note taped up in a rest area off the freeway near the Utah-Nevada border from a man trying to reach his family in Reno. He was out of gas and had no money. "If you can help me, I am sleeping in the gray Ford," the note finished. "God bless you."

Lois saw the car immediately, an old dilapidated car, all its windows open in the heat. A German shepherd was asleep on the sidewalk in a tiny patch of shade. The dog looked exhausted too. Lois felt sympathetic, but she also felt cynical. She wondered if the note writer was just trying to make money, and she realized that she didn't like thinking that way about someone else.

Other people were already helping. The man really didn't want money—just gas. Another traveler with a gas can contributed a couple of gallons of gas. The mother of three little children poured some ice chips into a bowl for the appreciative dog. An elderly man and his wife in a battered old car gave him a couple of dollars.

Then Lois writes: "As we walked back to our cars, I asked the elderly man if he ever worried about being 'taken.'

"'Nope,' he said. 'I just bought myself a good feeling. Cheap. If he's taking advantage of me, that's his problem, not

mine.'" ("A Little Compassion Buys a Great Feeli~~
News, Aug. 11–12, 1992, A11.)

Lois tells another story. A colleague at her office h~~
leaving an event with her children when she saw a ~~
pulling a wagon filled with miscellaneous household items
and panhandling. With shame, the friend confessed, "I did my
very best not to see them. If I didn't see them, I wouldn't have
to respond." Once in the car, however, she started to cry. She'd
always thought of herself as a kind person. She was stunned
to realize that she had ignored someone in obvious need.
She'd always tried to teach her children to help others. And
what was the message she'd just given them?

She insisted that they try to find the couple. It took them
about fifteen minutes of driving around the area before they
found them. The couple were missionaries who had given up
everything to come to America and had no money. Lois's
friend and her husband pressed all the money they had with
them into their hands, and then she kept on crying all the way
home. She was feeling the pain of realizing her own capacity
for hardheartedness.

Lois summarizes: "I could offer that bowl of ice chips. The
gallon of gas. The few small bills or coins. . . . And if I was
taken, I'd be out a bowl of ice chips. A gallon of gas. A few
small bills or coins. Big deal.

"What I can't afford to be out of is the feeling I am part of
a giving, caring world." (Ibid.)

I love these experiences. They exemplify the principle of
giving bread and fish instead of stones and scorpions. We can
give that kind of gentle, loving service to others. We can pour
ice chips into a bowl for a thirsty dog. We can hand a hungry

man a couple of dollars. We can listen sympathetically to a sister with a burden on her heart. We can sit next to a new sister and say, "I'm so glad you're here." And when we do, we receive the reward of a disciple. The reward of a disciple is that great big glow in the heart that turns into a great big smile, like the one I saw on my husband's face.

PATIENCE

The third principle that I want to talk about in relation to making Christ the foundation of our lives is patience. There's a lovely scripture in Isaiah that says, "Therefore thus saith the Lord God, Behold, I lay in Zion for a foundation a stone, a tried stone, a precious corner stone, a sure foundation: he that believeth shall not make haste." (Isaiah 28:16.) Now, who is this tried stone, the precious corner stone, the sure foundation? Yes, it's Christ. But what does the next part mean: "he that believeth shall not make haste"?

I think it means that we can build our household of faith slowly and carefully, "line upon line, precept upon precept" (D&C 128:21), knowing that every small effort counts, every small improvement is important, every cup of cold water is measured unto God. It means that we don't need to compare ourselves to anyone else. We don't need to keep checklists of our righteousness or be anxious or frantic about our lives. We are okay, just the way we are, each of us, with our own needs, our own abilities, our own desires for righteousness, and our own set of obstacles to overcome. When we build for eternity, we need not make haste.

Another reason for being patient with ourselves is that we cannot see the end from the beginning, as God can. Remember how a cat's cradle works? We don't know whose lives are going to touch ours at one point, then go off, loop back, and touch us in another way. During the summer of 1992, at a women's conference in Huntington Beach, Betty Martin introduced me to the congregation by saying, "Fifty years ago, my uncle Edward labored as a missionary in Hawaii where he learned to love the Japanese people. Soon after World War II broke out, his mission ended and he came back to the mainland where he joined the Air Force. He was very worried, thinking that he was going to be forced to fight against the Japanese people whom he loved so much. But during training, his plane crashed and he was killed. This was very hard for my grandmother and my mother, but it was a comfort, too, because we knew that he didn't have to kill anyone. Then when we were reading his missionary journal, we came across a reference to Chieko Nishimura on the big island of Hawaii—"

You can imagine that I suddenly sat up very straight with my eyes wide open. This was Elder Edward Cornelius, *my* Elder Cornelius, one of the elders who taught me the gospel when I was fifteen. I'd been an investigator since I was eleven, but he and his companion used to walk out to our little village of Mahukona, twelve or thirteen miles from Kohala, where they lived. It took so long for them to get there that my mother often had them sleep overnight at our house.

A few weeks later, Sister Martin sent me a very precious document—a photocopy of the pages of her uncle's diary where he talks about visiting our home. It's quite a strange feeling to read a missionary's diary and come across your own name there! What he said brought back so many details.

Elder Cornelius talked about working in a "switch-room,"

sometimes for up to seven hours. I'm not sure what this means, unless the missionaries were helping to fill in at the telephone switchboard at the police station in Kohala. He and his companion played basketball with the boys at my high school. They worked very hard holding Sunday School in three separate places each week plus MIA on Saturday nights. They were so pleased, he wrote, when eighteen people came to meeting.

Then the entry for Tuesday, January 13, 1942, reads: "This afternoon we went up to Mrs. Sakai's home and held our Cottage M[eeting]. Chieko Nishimura came over to the Meeting for the first time. She works right near there, but has been unable to attend before because of school. Had a nice meeting. We are expecting to have both of them in the Church before long."

It turns out he was right! On February 17, 1942, the mission president and one of the district leaders came through, so the missionaries took him to a cottage meeting at Sister Sakai's in Kokoike, which was about halfway to Mahukona. Elder Cornelius wrote, "Pres. Jensen gave us all some fine advice." I remember attending that meeting. I'd hitched a ride there. I still remember what a sweet man President Jensen was and how lovingly he expressed his appreciation for being with us. He knew our background and knew we would have challenges, but I remember his blessing that we would be able to keep the love of Christ in our heart. It was raining when the meeting ended, and I remember that we all had to walk back to Kohala six miles in a tropical rainstorm!

Then on Saturday, March 8, 1942, Elder Cornelius wrote: "This morning after breakfast we did the dishes and then cleaned the house a little bit. We then got ready to go to

Mahukona. . . . We had got as far as Kokoike when the air raid signal came on." After the all clear, they walked the rest of the way to our house. I was glad to read the next sentence: "Had a nice visit with the Nishimura family," he wrote.

I remember it all. Sister Sakai and I were baptized together not quite a month later—on April 6, 1942, to be exact. Elder Cornelius was transferred before that day, so he wasn't there. In fact, nobody was there except for the two missionaries, Sister Sakai, and me. I'm so grateful to Betty Martin for introducing herself to me, not only renewing my connection with Elder Cornelius but also making a new connection between her and me. I'm thankful Elder Cornelius and his companion had the patience to walk the thirteen miles out to Mahukona to visit a fifteen-year-old girl and encourage her to keep on studying the gospel. I'm so grateful for the two missionaries who spent the day filling with a hose the redwood box that served as a font where Sister Sakai and I were baptized. I'm thankful for those dear, generous-hearted Hawaiian sisters in the little branch in Mahukona. They scooted over and made room for a shy, skinny, eleven-year-old Japanese Buddhist next to their own children. They shared their hymnals with me. They patiently showed me how to read music. They took me with them when the women separated for Relief Society.

I'm thankful for all of the people who have been patient with me since then as I learned the gospel, those who gave Ed and me and our boys opportunities to serve, and those who are patient in sharing their stories and ministering to me now so that I can understand better the needs of the women of the Church. We do not need to be hasty. We can be patient. We are sisters in Zion, building on a foundation stone, a tried stone, a precious cornerstone, a sure foundation—the testimony of our Savior.

CONCLUSION

All of us, as members of the Church and as brothers and sisters in the gospel, are co-workers now with each other and with the Savior in the great cause of Christ—the cause of building the household of faith, the cause of bringing souls to him. Let us make him *our* way, *our* truth, *our* life.

First, let us make faith in him the foundation and cornerstone of our lives so that we can build the household of faith in power and love. The rains will fall and the floods will come up, but our house will stand if it is built on his rock.

Second, let us remember that Christ's way is the way of kindness. He does not ask of us things we cannot do; but if we will listen to our hearts, we will hear the whisper, "Give the dog some ice chips," or, as my husband heard the whisper, "This man needs a jacket more than you do." The kindness itself is a gift, no matter what gift it may accompany.

And third, we need not be hasty or run faster than we have strength. When we build for eternity, we have no time to waste, but we can take as much time as we need. We can lighten up about our work because Christ is our yokefellow in pulling the load. We can be patient with our little part of the pattern because we know our Heavenly Father knows the whole pattern. We can concentrate on making each encounter a positive one, each relationship a nurturing one, each contact a loving one—because we never know whose life will come back into contact with ours as the strands touch and cross and form new patterns.

CHAPTER 4

Beyond Juggling:
The Christian Life

I suspect that most women in the Church are expert jugglers. All of us have to deal with the perennial problem of finding time for family, church, self, and perhaps work. I've done a lot of juggling myself—including real juggling, the kind you do with oranges or balls—and the first thing that happened was pieces flying all over, totally out of control.

Sometimes we feel that we live in pieces. The Young Women owns a piece of us, our boss or daily responsibilities own a piece of us, the cancer drive owns a piece of us, the bishop comes along and takes a few more pieces, and every lesson and sacrament meeting talk we hear reminds us of more we should be doing or doing differently, and then more chunks of us sail off into feeling guilty and ashamed because we're not doing better.

When you see jugglers on television or in programs—I mean, people who really know how to juggle—they seem relaxed. It looks easy. They can talk while they're doing it. Their hands just seem to be in the right place at the right time. What is their secret? Why is it so easy for them and so hard for us?

The lesson of any juggling act is that sooner or later you drop the balls; sooner or later someone jiggles your elbow. Juggling is a marvelous, awe-inspiring performance because it defies belief. It defies reality. It defies the odds. But it's not a comfortable, normal way to live.

As I think about juggling, I keep coming back to the Savior. He was so busy, so pressed with responsibilities that he had to hide sometimes even to find time to pray, but we never think of his life as being out of control. We don't see pieces of his life flying away. We never think of him as distracted, interrupted, forgetting things, putting things down on lists and then forgetting where he put the list. We don't think of him as a juggler, although in many ways he must have been. How did Jesus *do* it? And is it possible that we could do it the same way Jesus did?

I think we can. And I'd like to share with you a powerful idea that I've drawn from Jesus' life. It is to create an integrated identity, a Christian identity. A Christian identity is a powerful principle that lets us live with the *parts* of our lives integrated into the *whole* of our lives. Then I'd like to discuss some of the consequences of having an integrated Christian identity. The first consequence is that we can stop juggling. We can stop switching roles, snatching and grabbing at minutes of time, and moving nervously from task to task. It lets us be centered in Christ and stand firm and calm. The second consequence is that it lets us live in the present, so that depression about the past and worry about the future do not rob our present of its joy and vitality. And the third consequence is that it lets us act with deep confidence in ourselves and in the Lord.

AN INTEGRATED CHRISTIAN IDENTITY

So how do we begin? For me, the unifying principle is to be a follower of Christ, a disciple of Christ, a sister of Christ everywhere I am, no matter where I am, no matter who I am with, and no matter what I am doing.

Remember how the scriptures describe the great council in heaven? Jesus stood before the Father and said, "Here am I; send me." (Abraham 3:27.) Mary, kneeling before the angel Gabriel, said, "Behold the handmaid of the Lord; be it unto me according to thy word." (Luke 1:38.) These are life-integrating statements. They pull all of the parts together into something solid and whole.

We know from the rest of Jesus' mortal life that he drew great strength from that commitment, from being able to say, "Here am I; send me." We know less about Mary's life, but she could not have had the strength to raise her Son, send him forth, listen to the reports of both the miracles and the mockery, and then stand steadfast at the foot of the cross if she had not drawn great strength from that life-integrating statement, "Behold the handmaid of the Lord."

For me, great strength comes every week as I partake of the sacrament and remind myself that I bear the name of Christ, that I have taken it upon myself like something tangible. Sometimes, when I am feeling lonely and tired, I take the name of the Savior upon me like a warm blanket. I wrap myself in it the way my two-year-old grandson wraps himself in his cherished "blankey," and I feel warmed and comforted. If I am feeling vulnerable, sometimes I take the name of Christ upon me like armor, feeling it solid and bright and impregnable, so that no opposition can puncture it and so that no wound can devastate me. Sometimes I take the name of Christ upon me like Joseph's coat of many colors, a beautiful garment in which to dance and rejoice and praise the Lord.

I don't know how you remind yourself that you are a Christian, bearing the name of your King and Savior. But maybe it will help you to think of something like this example of mine. Find your own life-integrating statement to remind you who you are and what holds your life together.

Our lives are full of voices trying to tell us who we are. Television advertisements try to talk us into being consumers of this product or that product. Newspapers and magazines publish editorials that try to sway us from one position to another. We read opinion polls and think, "Am I for this issue or against that one?" We each have many roles that our life circumstances bring: student, parent, spouse, employee, teacher in the church, administrator in the church, divorcee, widow or widower, boss, neighbor, temple worker, family historian, community worker, volunteer, reader, writer, recycler . . . Why, the list simply doesn't end.

All of these roles can turn into brightly colored balls, flying through the air at us. Each one can claim to be the most important one, the one we should drop all the other balls for. That can happen to us even in the Church. One of my missionaries told me that he was called to be the elders quorum president soon after he married. Along with the handbook, the high council had also supplied a typed list of "The Twenty-Two Most Important Responsibilities You Must Do Every Week." Fortunately he had a good sense of humor. Through studying the handbook, through talking with the elders in his ward, and through diligently seeking inspiration, he and his counselors set priorities to meet the needs of the men in the quorum.

I don't think we can have an integrated, Christ-centered life unless we take all the parts of our lives to him, spread them out before him, and let him heal them into one Christ-centered whole. When he does, we receive our lives back again from the Savior, sanctified by the Holy Ghost, radiant with grace. What does that mean—to take our lives to Jesus and to receive sanctified lives from him again? Jesus knew who he was. He said, "I am the bread of life" (John 6:35); "I am the light of the world" (John 8:12); "I am the good shepherd" (John 10:11); "I am the resurrection, and the life" (John 11:25); "I am the way, the truth, and the life" (John 14:6); "I am the vine, ye are the branches" (John 15:5).

Did you notice that three of those statements used the word *life?* Christ defined himself as life. Perhaps the most important life-integrating statement he made about his mission here on the earth was, "I am come that they might have life, and that they might have it more abundantly." (John 10:10.)

What is the kind of life he wants us to have? He wants us to have *him, his* life, *his* way of living. And isn't that what we want? Isn't sharing in the life and will and works of Jesus what we all hunger and thirst for?

But wait, you might say. Our lives aren't the same. We don't know much about Jesus' life before he turned thirty, and then he was on a full-time mission. During his three-year ministry, he depended on the charity of friends and strangers for food, clothing, and shelter. He did not have direct responsibility for a wife and children. He did not work at a profession after he began his ministry. Sometimes we think, That would be great, but I've got three teenagers, a son on a mission, a mother in the rest home, the Laurel class, and I'm in charge of the school carnival. Who will take care of them while I go about doing good, like Jesus?

Living a Christ-centered life doesn't mean that all of those responsibilities are in competition with being Christian. Jesus wants us to take all of those parts of our lives to him in prayer, lay them out before him, and ask him to be with us in all of these responsibilities. In other words, Jesus doesn't want us to go about doing good; he wants us to *stay put* doing good. This is what being an every-day Christian means. It doesn't mean that you're one person at work, and then you hurry home and are another person making a batch of brownies for the school bake sale, and then you hurry to teach your Laurel class where you turn into a third person and hope there's some time left over for you to be a Christian. It means being a Christian, being a Latter-day Saint *while* you're at work, *while* you're making the brownies, *while* you're at the Laurel class. Sometimes we think Jesus doesn't really understand any of the parts of our lives except our families and our Church jobs. Well, he created the world. He knows exactly what living in the world means. And when we take his name upon us, it means that we can have a life integrated around our identity as a Christian. Thus, we can be Christians no matter where we are or what we're doing or who we're with.

What happens if you think of yourself as a total Christian? It means that you're in disguise on a secret mission for God. Your secret mission is to provide love and service for people that Jesus would have served if he were here on the earth.

Every person you are with is the person Jesus wants you to serve, whether that's your four-year-old child, your eighty-year-old auntie, the counselors in the bishopric meeting, the fourteen-year-olds in your Sunday School class, the tourist who asks you for directions, the children you are carpooling to school, or the secretary you ask to type a letter. These people may be family or they may be strangers, but they are the neighbors Jesus wants you to serve. And they may think, "Oh, that's Mom, that's the teacher, that's the boss," but really, those roles are the temporary disguises you put on to conceal your real identity as a Christian.

THE JUGGLING STOPS

Now let's talk about some of the consequences of seeing yourself first, foremost, and always as a Christian. The first consequence is that the juggling stops. If you think of all your tasks, jobs, and roles as balls that you somehow have to keep in the air, then your religious service is just another ball to add. Sooner or later, you're going to drop the balls, because no one can juggle forever. But if you are a Christian, then that is your permanent identity and everything else is temporary. Think of this example. You dash into the grocery store to pick up some ice cream for supper. You're a harried mom, a frantic shopper, eager to get in and get out. Other people are in your way—the person stocking the shelves, the people ahead of you in the checkout line, the checker. You're even more frazzled when you reach the car.

But suppose you go in as a Christian disguised as a shopper. You see other people on your way to the ice cream, excuse yourself and smile when you reach past the person stocking the shelves, comment on the weather to the person standing in front of you at the checkout stand, and thank the checker who whisks the ice cream into a bag for you. You reach the car having had three very pleasant encounters and feeling good.

If we see every place, every job, every responsibility as an opportunity to be with another precious child of God who needs our ministry, the ministry we can bring as a Christian and as a disciple of Christ, then even a very busy schedule doesn't feel like juggling any more. Something has taken the fragmentation out of it and given us a unified purpose.

My husband, Ed, was this kind of Christian, an every-day Christian, even an every-minute Christian. Sometimes we think that the life of a disciple is hard, but if you knew Ed, you would know that it is a joyous, rewarding life. Terms like *hard* or *easy* really didn't make sense to Ed. When he was doing what Christ did—helping and serving other people—his life was filled to overflowing with joy and love. Nothing made him happier than finding something to do for someone else. He didn't make rules for himself like, "Take the children in your home teaching families out for ice cream cones when it's their birthday." He didn't need to make rules for himself because he was sincerely interested in each child, had written down their names and birth dates on his very first visit, and was anxious to find a chance to give each child a treat. And each time he did, it made him so happy that he was more anxious to find something else to do for each person. In other words, Christian discipleship was its own reward, not something he had to drag himself to do by making rules for himself and exercising enormous willpower.

Sometimes I wonder what made Ed so good. I know that a

great part of it came from the good teachings he had received from his parents and his Congregationalist church. They taught him to love Jesus, to love the scriptures, and to do all the good he could to everyone. Ed never theorized about the gospel. He didn't try to systematize the theology, and he wasn't very interested, actually, in theoretical discussions about points of doctrine. He wanted to *live* the gospel as well as talk about it. He was hungry for the scriptures. One of my most enduring memories is seeing Ed sitting and reading his scriptures. He didn't read the scriptures because it was a commandment, or because his high priest quorum had set the goal of reading the Book of Mormon that year, or because he was preparing a lesson—although he took all of those obligations seriously. He was hungry to see how the gospel worked. He was thirsty for the words of the Savior. He was eager to learn more about how to be a better Christian.

Ed's companion was Christ. All of our life together, when we were discussing a situation or a problem, Ed would ask, "What would Christ do?" That made many decisions very simple and very clear, though sometimes they were not very easy to carry out. Over the years, I heard him ask this same question to young people, to struggling couples, to perplexed missionaries, to confused home teachees, and each time this question helped them find their own answers. In later years, Ed asked this question less often, and sometimes I heard him say, "I know what Christ would do." I think that Ed had been a faithful companion of Christ for so long that he could literally do the works that the Savior would have done. The apostle Paul has a lovely statement that I think applies to Ed: "For who hath known the mind of the Lord, that he may instruct him? But we have the mind of Christ." (1 Corinthians 2:16.) I think Ed had the mind of Christ.

Because Ed's identity was that of a disciple, he was free from many problems and vexations that are troublesome for other people. He never wasted any energy being angry at someone who had mistreated him. He never allowed his attention to be drawn into enmity or bitterness, even when bitter things happened. He never hated the Germans whose artillery fire wounded him and almost killed him. He never resented the people who mistrusted Japanese-American soldiers during World War II. I was always so proud of Ed. He reproached evil by his very being, because he was so good.

Because Ed had a disciple's identity, he did not need to make distinctions among people. In that way, I think he was like Mother Teresa. He saw the face of Christ in every human face. He never treated his boss in a way different from the way he treated the janitor. He behaved with the same cordiality toward the bishop and toward the fourteen-year-old Scout. When we went into sacrament meeting, he shook hands with the fathers, the mothers, the teenagers, and the children, right down to the babies.

Do you see how making a commitment to Heavenly Father and having a life-integrating identity can eliminate our feeling that we're juggling too many balls? One of the most difficult problems we struggle with is switching roles: here we're a mother, there we're a bishop, here we're an employee, there we're a Scoutmaster. If we're a different person in each of these roles, then a great deal of energy has to go into remembering which tone of voice to use, which manner to put on, and how to behave in each role. And what happens when the roles collide? When our family role suddenly overlaps with our employee role? If we're just one integrated person— if just one simple principle forms the foundation of our identity—much energy is freed for other things.

So that's the first consequence of having an integrated Christian identity. We can eliminate the juggling act. It lets us be the same person at all times and in all places. Then instead of fretting, worrying, and fumbling as we drop one role and pick up a new one, we can concentrate on our real task: serving whoever we are with.

LIVE IN THE MOMENT

The second consequence of having an integrated Christian identity is that it lets us develop a different sense of time. You know that one of the marvelous things about watching a juggler is how easy it looks. A juggler's hands move in a very precise rhythm but without being tense or jerky or nervous. Of course, a juggling act lasts only a few minutes, and we need to find a lifestyle that can go on much longer, so let's think about Jesus' sense of time.

I believe that Jesus was very conscious of time, but he was never in a hurry. He never said, "Don't you get it? I've only got three years. Listen up! Pay attention! Get that multitude fed right now! Get a move on. Snap it up. We've got to get to the walls of Jerusalem before the owner of the colt moves it." I think it's very interesting that the only time Jesus is recorded as saying, "Hurry up" was when he walked under the sycamore tree where a short tax collector named Zacchaeus had climbed so he could see Jesus. According to Luke: "And when Jesus came to the place, he looked up, and saw him, and

said unto him, Zacchaeus, make haste, and come down; for to
day I must abide at thy house." (Luke 19:5.) I don't think Jesus
told Zacchaeus to "make haste" because Jesus was in a hurry
but because he wanted Zacchaeus to act without saying, "Let's
see, do I really want this radical preacher in my house? How
does he know my name? Have some of my enemies put him
up to this?" In other words, Jesus wasn't in a hurry, but he
wanted Zacchaeus to be in a hurry to hear the words he
needed to understand so he could repent.

Jesus had a wonderful gift of living in the present
moment. He could pray as long as he needed to while his disciples were sailing across the Sea of Galilee, because he could
walk on the water, if he needed, to rejoin them. He could
preach an entire day to a multitude in the wilderness, because
he knew there would be sufficient bread and fish to feed them
when night came. When you stop to think of it, the present is
all we've got. We can predict and make guesses about the
future, but we can't control it. The past is already out of our
reach. If we can live each present moment without trying to
cling to it as it moves into the past, then, like the juggler, our
hands will be in the right place at the right time.

One woman wrote of a wonderful experience about learning to live in the moment. She had bought a "misbegotten
onion" for $5.95 and planted it in a soup tureen. It grew into a
"skinny houseplant," and then suddenly, one day when she
wasn't looking, it burst into a flamboyant, crimson flower. The
flower came so quickly that she knew it would also leave
quickly. "Now!" her flower demanded. "Now is the flame-
orange, crimson-trumpeted moment. Look *now!*" Of course,
she didn't want it to die. She stared at it until her eyes ached,

until she needed "a trip to the flatware drawer or a view of the dish towels. Something not so demanding." And it made her think. Should she have spent $5.95 on something as impermanent as an amaryllis? For $5.95, she could have bought "a durable stainless-steel spoon. . . . A spoon would last longer than an amaryllis. A lot of things would last longer than an amaryllis. However," she continued, "I own a drawerful of spoons. And not one of them in five years has given me as much happiness as the amaryllis has in one week."

She accepted her flower's death as unimportant. What was important was to have saluted its beauty and its vibrancy in living and the moment of joy that it gave her right then. (Debbie Anfenson-Vance, "Slipping through My Fingers All the Time," *Signs of the Times,* Aug. 1992, p. 11.)

Ed had the same gift of living in the moment. He was always on time and even early, but he was never in a hurry. I think perhaps he felt that his life was a gift. When Ed was eighteen, his father died very suddenly of a heart attack. His father was a young man, just forty years old, and he had not been ill. He was driving down a road on Maui, and by coincidence, the local police officer was driving behind him. He was driving very slowly, then more slowly still, and his car gently aimed toward the right side of the road and then, very slowly, came to a stop in the little ditch beside the road. The police officer parked and hurried to Ed's father, but he was already dead. Ed himself died in much the same way, although he had had many more years to live than his father. Ed felt that those years past forty were a gift, for he often said so.

He felt that his years after World War II were particularly a gift. He was a minesweeper, a terribly dangerous specialty.

Many of his friends in the 442d were killed, and he himself was severely wounded. He could very easily have been among the dead. And out of the bitterness and anger and hatred that war so often generates, Ed took only gratitude for his life, a great sweetness of disposition, and a complete generosity toward anyone whom he could help.

If we can be Christians, every day and every minute, then we can live in the present without letting worries about the future or regrets about the past drag us down. I think we will find that there is enough time to do every task beautifully and rejoice in it and to feel the joy and love that comes from focusing on people instead of on jobs and things.

HAVING CONFIDENCE

The third consequence of having an integrated Christian identity is that it lets us act with deep confidence in ourselves and in the Lord. The very best jugglers—not me!—don't look nervous and tense. They look relaxed and easy. They know they can do it. So often, we feel nervous and tense because we feel inadequate, incapable, and unsure of ourselves.

Think about the Savior. It takes a lot of confidence to tell a blind man to see, or to tell a crippled man to pick up his bed, or to set off walking across the surface of a stormy sea. Where did Jesus' confidence come from? I think it came from his relationship with his Heavenly Father. If we have faith in the Savior and follow his example, I think that we also can have the same kind of confidence. Jesus taught us how to pray, how to approach our Father in Heaven in great confidence and great love. I have read that the Aramaic word Jesus used doesn't mean just "Father" but something much more intimate, like "Daddy" or "Papa," the word a very small child would use in calling to his or her father. The apostle Paul told the Hebrews: "Let us . . . come boldly unto the throne of grace, that we may obtain mercy, and find grace to help in time of need." (Hebrews 4:16.) Paul was reminding the Hebrews that they could have confidence in Christ because He was their Savior. He reminded the people that they were only mortals but they still were good enough to give bread and fish to their children, not stones or serpents. "How much more shall your heavenly Father give the Holy Spirit to them that ask him?" (Luke 11:13.)

Doesn't that increase our confidence that we can ask our Heavenly Father, confide our troubles in him, share our griefs and burdens, rejoice in his blessings, and step off in faith even if it looks as if we will be planting our feet on the stormy surface of unstable water?

When responsibilities seem to be falling upon us thick and fast, when our hands are already full but here comes something else, when people around us don't seem to understand, let's remember that our Heavenly Father *does* understand, that the simple confidence Jesus had in his Father is the same confidence that we can have in him.

CONCLUSION

I probably haven't given you many hints about how to juggle all of your responsibilities better. Instead, I have tried to share with you a different way of seeing ourselves—not as jugglers but as brothers and sisters of Christ, his disciples and his co-workers. Juggling means that we always have to keep our eye on the next ball coming and our hands moving. We're locked into a rhythm that will bring everything toppling down on us if we make the slightest mistake. I don't think that the Christian life is as much like juggling as it is like hearing music and joining our voice in its chorus, even when we don't know the words perfectly, or like joining in a dance, even if we don't know the steps perfectly.

We reach this new way of seeing ourselves by centering our lives on Christ, by taking our lives to him, laying them out before him in prayer, and then receiving them back from him sanctified. He wants us to be parents, children, students, bosses, employees, community workers, church workers. All of those roles give us experiences that bring us into contact with other beloved children of God. But he wants us to act in all of those roles as his disciples, as every-minute Christians. That orientation is a powerful principle that lets us live a life in which the parts are integrated into the whole.

And we've also talked about three consequences. First, the juggling stops. We see ourselves differently. We can act with integrity and authenticity no matter where we are or who we are with. The second consequence is that we can live in the present, so that depression about the past and worry about the future do not rob our present of its joy and vitality. And the third consequence is that we can act with confidence, not with insecurity and doubt.

Let me conclude with the powerful words of the Savior to the Saints of Joseph Smith's day:

> Pray always, and I will pour out my Spirit upon you, and great shall be your blessing—yea, even more than if you should obtain treasures of earth and corruptibleness to the extent thereof.

Behold, canst thou read this without re
up thy heart for gladness?

Or canst thou run about longer as a bli

Or canst thou be humble and meek, an
wisely before me? Yea, come unto me
19:38–41)

CHAPTER 5

Keeping a Balance

What do you see in your mind's eye when you hear the phrase "keeping a balance"? Do you see the fiddler on the roof, balancing across the ridgepole as he plays his violin? Do you see an exquisite gymnast working with elegance and precision on a balance beam? Do you see the traditional statue of Justice, blindfolded and holding in her hand her scales to weigh the balance of evidence between truth and error, justice and injustice? One of Job's prayers was "Let me be weighed in an even balance, that God may know mine integrity." (Job 31:6.)

Do you know the children's game "Spill the Beans," in which a little platform is balanced at two points? Each player must add a bean to the platform. Because it's balanced at only two points, it's very unstable, so if the beans begin to pile up on one side, it begins to tip. The person who adds the bean that makes the platform tip and spill the beans loses the game.

Sometimes our lives feel like that—everyone has a bean to add to our platform, we can feel things getting lopsided and out of control, but—whoops! here comes another bean and there goes the whole pile, spilling all over the place.

When it comes to keeping balance in our lives, I want to suggest a simple technique: find the center of balance and strengthen that point until it has enough solidity and weight that it doesn't matter if things are a little out of balance on top. For example, most trees are naturally symmetrical, if they're allowed to grow with access on all sides to the same amount of sun, wind, and soil. But sometimes a tree is close to a house, so it has lots of branches on one side but not very many on the other. Sometimes, like on the windward side of Hawaii, the wind blows steadily for most of the year from one direction, so the tree bends under that wind, pointing inland. Sometimes a tree is too close to another tree, so that it grows in a curve, seeking an open space where it can get more sunlight.

We don't think of these trees as sick or handicapped or dysfunctional. We don't even think of them as out of balance, even though they are no longer symmetrical. They're healthy and functional and will do just fine for years. Why? Because it's not the branches on the right that have to balance the branches on the left. The point of balance is between the branches and the roots. If the roots are sturdy and run deep into the soil, then the tree as a whole is strong and healthy and in balance.

Think of the image of the tree, not the image of the spilling beans or the image of the scales of justice. Our lives as women often require that we grow thicker branches on one side of our lives than another. There are seasons of mothering when almost all of our energy goes into those branches. There are seasons of serving a mission or serving in an intensive calling when those branches grow thick and bushy. There are times of completing an academic program or establishing a career. During those times, one part of the tree gets most of the growth. But the tree as a whole will stay in balance if the roots are deep and healthy.

What are the roots in our lives that give us this kind of health and stability? It's our relationship with the Savior. Paul pronounced an extraordinary blessing upon the Ephesian Saints:

> For this cause I bow my knees unto the Father of our Lord Jesus Christ, . . .
> That Christ may dwell in your hearts by faith; that ye, *being rooted and grounded in love,*
> May be able to comprehend with all saints what is the breadth, and length, and depth, and height;
> And to know the love of Christ, which passeth knowledge, that ye might be filled with all the fulness of God. (Ephesians 3:14, 17–19; emphasis added)

If you felt "rooted and grounded in love," wouldn't it be easier to feel balance in yourself? Wouldn't you be able to put out new branches in areas where you need them? Wouldn't you feel a stronger ability to stay focused on the important parts of your life? Wouldn't it be easier to set priorities and make decisions?

Of course it would. As Paul explained to the Romans, "If the root be holy, so are the branches." (Romans 11:16.) So let's discuss how to find a balance by sinking deep roots in our relationship with Christ. Then let's consider how to use that strength to meet our own needs and the needs of others.

ROOTING OURSELVES IN CHRIST

I'm not going to tell you to read the scriptures, fast and pray, keep the commandments, attend the temple, and attend your meetings as ways of coming to know Christ. We all know that those things are important, and we know why they're important. All of them will improve and strengthen our relationship with the Savior, but they are *not* the relationship itself, and sometimes we forget that. The relationship I'm talking about is a sense of presence, a sense of companionship, a sense of closeness. It's a relationship not with an idea or a historical image but with a living individual. When we have the feeling of the Savior as a real person, there's a new awareness of what it means to take his name upon us, almost of being clothed in his name, of seeing with his eyes and of feeling his work being done with our hands.

I want to relate two stories that will, I hope, give you a feeling of what this new reality feels like. The first story is about Mother Teresa, told not by herself but by a rather skeptical—an agnostic—television journalist named Malcolm Muggeridge, who did some prizewinning documentaries. He remembers his first meeting with Mother Teresa as really nothing extraordinary. He was doing a television interview with her for the BBC. He knew nothing about her beyond a few facts that he had hastily read in the train on the way to London. He writes:

> I sat waiting for her, with appropriate questions running through my head; the camera, the lights, the sound recordist, all in position. A scene desolatingly familiar to me. Then she came in. It was, for me, one of those special occasions when a face, hitherto unknown, seems to stand out from all other faces as uniquely separate and uniquely significant. . . . I knew that, even if I were never to see Mother Teresa again, the memory of her would stay with me for ever.

Still, the interview was only ordinary. Mother Teresa did not play to the camera or utter scintillating one-liners. When he asked her provocative questions, she simply responded with thoughtful sincerity, giving answers that were exactly what you would expect from a nun with an Albanian accent. She did not seem to recognize controversial subjects and certainly did not follow up on them. At the end, there was considerable dissatisfaction among the BBC personnel. As Muggeridge described it:

> The verdict on the Mother Teresa interview was that, technically, it was barely usable, and there was for a while some doubt as to whether it was good enough for showing at all except late at night. In the end . . . it was put out on a Sunday evening. The response was greater than I have known to any comparable programme, both in mail and in contributions of money for Mother Teresa's work. I myself received many letters enclosing cheques and money-orders ranging between a few shillings and hundreds of pounds. They came from young and old, rich and poor, educated and uneducated; all sorts and conditions of people. All of them said approximately the same thing—this woman spoke to me as no one ever has, and I feel I must help her. . . .
>
> The Mother Teresa programme was repeated quite soon after its first showing in response to numerous requests, and the response to the repeat programme was even greater than to the original one. Altogether, something like 20,000 pounds found its way to . . . Mother Teresa.

Then Malcolm Muggeridge asks the question that we are surely asking ourselves:

> Why? Why would an obscure nun of Albanian origins, very nervous . . . in front of the camera, somewhat halting in speech, . . . reach English viewers on a Sunday evening as no professional Christian . . . bishop or archbishop . . . ever has? But this is exactly what happened, to the surprise of all professionally concerned, including me. The message

was the same message that was heard in the world for the first time two thousand years ago; as Mother Teresa showed, it has not changed or lost its magic. As then, so now, it is brought, not with enticing words of man's wisdom, but in demonstration of the Spirit and of power; that your faith should not stand in the wisdom of men, but in the power of God. (*Something Beautiful for God: Mother Teresa of Calcutta* [New York: Walker and Co./Phoenix Press, 1971; large print ed., 1984), pp. 13, 20–23)

In other words, this mysterious magic that Mother Teresa conveyed, this remarkable appeal, had very little to do with her at all. She was simply a pure-hearted woman through whom the miraculous message of the Master moved and looked out, comforting the sorrow and feeding the hunger of those who were perishing for lack of spiritual nourishment. People wanted to be with Mother Teresa, to help her in her work, and to follow her because they felt the Spirit of Christ in her. She was "rooted and grounded" in the love of Christ. Those roots were so strong and healthy that she was an immensely happy, contented, and nurturing woman despite what must have been an extremely stressful lifestyle, what looks like an extreme lack of balance between the important value, to us, of family life and Christian service, very few material resources, and the kinds of needs and demands on her time and resources that make our little platforms piled with beans seem almost trivial by comparison.

Some people may feel that they can't relate to Mother Teresa. Our family-centered lives, our social and professional responsibilities, and many of our beliefs seem so different. It's true: they are. But her attachment to the Savior is something that we can all relate to and feel the power of.

The second story occurs in a more familiar context. I recently attended a Relief Society regional conference in Washington, D.C., and on Sunday I was given my choice of wards and branches to attend. I chose an inner-city branch, Mount Pleasant First Branch, and there I saw the fulfillment of the Savior's promise, "Where two or three are gathered together in my name, there am I in the midst of them." (Matthew 18:20.)

The teacher warmly greeted everyone. Members of the class were talking among themselves with affection and concern and pleasure at being together. It was obvious that Sunday School class was a warm and welcoming place to be; the people were there because they wanted to be. I was a stranger, but I felt the sense of love they all shared because it reached out and enveloped me, too.

The lesson was on honesty in human relations, and the teacher talked about interdependence as an ideal state, whereas dependence and independence both created unhealthy relations. When she started talking about interdependence, a toothless and shabbily dressed woman on the front row raised her hand and said, "I disagree. No such thing as interdependence. Who pays my rent if I don't? Nobody. And I'm going to jail."

The teacher asked, "How do you know you're going to jail?"

"Because I've been there before," retorted the woman. "I've got some money coming next week, but it won't help, and nobody helps me."

"I can help you," said the teacher. "I'm an attorney; and if you've got money coming in, then there's a way to arrange for the payment."

"You can help me?" exclaimed the woman, jumping up. "You can really help me?"

"Just as soon as the lesson is over," said the teacher.

"When?" demanded the woman. "When can you help me?" Confused and insistent, she repeated her question again. It was clear she was disrupting the lesson. I looked around me at the faces of the class members. No one showed impatience or embarrassment or irritation. They all looked upon this woman kindly. In their total acceptance, I felt again the Spirit of the Savior.

The teacher left her books and blackboard and walked to the row where this woman was talking, loudly repeating her question. She put her arms around the woman and explained again, slower and more clearly, "I can help you in ten minutes," she said. In most wards I have been in, someone would have taken the woman out of the room or those around would have given her rebuking looks. But in the faces of those in that simple room, I saw only kindness. No one was angry at her. No one was embarrassed that she was making a disturbance in front of a visitor from Salt Lake.

The woman quieted immediately, looked into the teacher's face, and said, "Can I sit by you until the meeting is over?" So the teacher gave her a chair right beside the table and continued with the lesson. After six or seven minutes, the woman became restless again, shifting in her chair, gesturing to a missionary on the front row, and pointing at her wrist, obviously asking whether the time was up. I couldn't see what the missionary did, but again the teacher calmed her by touching her and speaking to her directly.

Again I looked at the faces of the class members. I saw

only love and acceptance. I will always remember that woman, that teacher, and that lesson. We were all learning the real lesson—"Inasmuch as ye have done it unto one of the least of these, my [children], ye have done it unto me." (Matthew 25:40.) I wanted to weep from the sheer beauty of this Christian community acting in love.

In Relief Society, the president, a radiantly happy Hispanic woman, was conducting the opening exercises, her face so joyful as she welcomed the sisters that I could feel the attachment and kinship. I can't tell you how thoroughly at home I felt. A black woman offered a simple opening prayer that truly cried unto the Lord. I knew that she knew to whom she was talking. The Relief Society room was the first room off the hallway. A man who seemed slightly retarded wandered in, looking somewhat confused, and started to sit down. Without any constraint or embarrassment, the Relief Society president greeted him by name and gently reminded him where the priesthood meeting was being held.

As sacrament meeting began, the counselor in the bishopric who was conducting, a Caucasian, began opening exercises, but unexpectedly his voice broke with emotion. He was surprised. He apologized, "I don't know why I feel this way. It doesn't have anything to do with what I'm saying." But I knew what he was feeling. It was the spirit of love that had filled that little rented chapel from the moment that branch had convened that morning. It was one of the most precious experiences of my life. I did not want to leave. The Lord was there with us.

Think of your own experiences with that sweet, unmistakable spirit. Under the influence of that spirit, it is easy to be patient, kind, loving, and strong. It is easy to be brave, clear, and resourceful. It is easy to reach out to others, to protect yourself and your children, to feel contentment with your circumstances, to act on impulses of generosity whether you have much or little, to perceive quickly and perceptively a heart that is breaking with sorrow, and to find in yourself the healing word and the tender touch with which to meet that need.

In general conference President Howard W. Hunter quoted the words of the hymn "Jesus, the Very Thought of Thee" (*Hymns* [Salt Lake City: The Church of Jesus Christ of Latter-day Saints, 1985], no. 141.) and talked of the miraculous power of thoughts of Jesus. The words of this hymn are a Christian expression of faith and desire that is almost nine hundred years old. President Hunter said: "Surely life would be more peaceful, surely marriages and families would be stronger, certainly neighborhoods and nations would be safer and kinder and more constructive if more of the gospel of Jesus Christ 'with sweetness' could fill our breasts." He expressed the hope that such thoughts would fill our hearts, that we could hope "to claim that greater joy, that sweeter prize: someday his loving 'face to see / And in [his] presence rest.' . . .

". . . Is there one among us, in any walk of life, who does not need hope and seek for greater joy? These are the universal needs and longings of the human soul, and they are the promises of Christ to his followers."

President Hunter continued: "Sooner or later, and we pray sooner *than* later, everyone will acknowledge that Christ's way is not only the *right* way, but ultimately the *only* way to hope and joy. Every knee shall bow and every tongue will confess that gentleness is better than brutality, that kindness is greater than coercion, that the soft voice turneth away wrath. In the end, and sooner than that whenever possible, we must be more like him." ("Jesus, the Very Thought of Thee," *Ensign,* May 1993, pp. 64–65.)

Remember the sweet, sweet spirit that comes with our awareness of our Savior. It's this feeling I want you to remember when we talk about keeping a balance in our life. We're not trying to balance reading the scriptures against making a casserole for the ward dinner, or visiting teaching against serving on a PTA committee, or earning money to keep a missionary son or daughter in the field against writing a family history. We're not trying to balance the Savior or our spiritual life against any other aspect of our life. The Savior is the fulcrum of the balance, the pivot point of the balance, the trunk and roots of the tree that keep the branches in balance. We're trying to keep this feeling about the Savior sweet and strong, because then, questions of priorities and how to spend our time will be easy and clear.

In Proverbs 8, God says:

> I love them that love me; and those that seek me early shall find me.
>
> Riches and honour are with me; yea, durable riches and righteousness.
>
> My fruit is better than gold, yea, than fine gold; and my revenue than choice silver....
>
> ... I ... cause those that love me to inherit substance; and I will fill their treasures. (Proverbs 8:17–21)

To his disciples, Jesus said, "Seek ye first the kingdom of God, and his righteousness; and all these things shall be added unto you." (Matthew 6:33.) And where is the kingdom of God? When the Pharisees asked Jesus that question, he answered, "The kingdom of God cometh not with observation [meaning visibly, or with outward show]: Neither shall they say, Lo here! or, lo there! for, behold, the kingdom of God is within you." (Luke 17:20–21.) In other words, if we truly "come unto Christ" and "are rooted and grounded" in his love, we will find within ourselves the peace and strength to maintain balance in the rest of our lives.

That balance may be different for each one of us, depending on the needs and demands of those around us and the season of our life. What is balance for a young mother is different from what is balance for a single woman. What is balance for a healthy woman is different from what is balance for a chronically ill woman. What is balance for an attorney is different from what is balance for a teacher. But what is the same for each of those women is the need to find that balance in the Savior's love and strength and trust in her. That's a very personal relationship and a very personal search. Many others may have helpful counsel for you, but nobody else gets to make that decision for you.

When a Pharisee lawyer asked Jesus which commandment was the greatest, Jesus did not get drawn into a discussion of balancing the relative merits and importance of a complex law with many parts. Instead, he taught a doctrine that was simple and powerful:

> Thou shalt love the Lord thy God with all thy heart, and with all thy soul, and with all thy mind.
> This is the first and great commandment.
> And the second is like unto it, Thou shalt love thy neighbour as thyself.

On these two commandments hang all the law and the prophets. (Matthew 22:37–40)

That is the same commandment that Moses gave to the children of Israel before they entered the promised land:

Hear, O Israel: The Lord our God is one Lord:
And thou shalt love the Lord thy God with all thine heart, and with all thy soul, and with all thy might.
And these words, which I command thee this day, shall be in thine heart:
And thou shalt teach them diligently unto thy children, and shalt talk of them when thou sittest in thine house, and when thou walkest by the way, and when thou liest down, and when thou risest up.
And thou shalt bind them for a sign upon thine hand, and they shall be as frontlets between thine eyes.
And thou shalt write them upon the posts of thy house, and on thy gates. (Deuteronomy 6:4–9)

Now, what's so important about the teaching, the speaking, the signs, and the writing on the gate posts? Nothing at all—in themselves. All of those pious rules and observances existed for one reason: to help the people of Israel learn to love the Lord. They could do all of those things and never love the Lord or do all of those things instead of loving the Lord.

Sometimes we fill our lives with pious rules and observances too, or let other people do it for us. We forget the Lord. We forget to love him. We forget to feel in our hearts his love for us. And that's when our lives get out of balance, when our trees come crashing down in a windstorm because the roots are shallow, or when our little platform gets overbalanced and spills the beans we have balanced so busily and so carefully on it.

When our hearts are centered on the Savior, we don't have to drag ourselves to do good works. They spring up generously and abundantly. They don't fatigue us or frighten us or drain our energy. They give us energy. They make us want to do more. And simultaneously, we become less attached to what we do because we see that it is truly the Savior working through us. I think of people like Ray Ertmann, a Scoutmaster. One of his Scouts, Lester W. B. Moore, who later became president of the Polynesian Cultural Center in Hawaii, said that Brother Ertmann had a wonderful influence in his life because he was such a loving and available man. "His house was always open to us. He said, 'As long as the front porch light is on, you can come in and see me.' [And Brother Ertmann] left the light on all night every night." (Gerry Avant, "No Longer a Stranger in Paradise," *Church News*, 18 July 1992, p. 11.)

I think of the pure-hearted and loving service of Tony and Angie Franquelli and their two children, eleven-year-old Anthony and thirteen-year-old Jilleien. At a family home evening in April 1991 they decided they wanted to "do something in the community to help the kids learn compassion" and also to build "a lot of family unity." Anthony suggested they feed the homeless, so they bought some extra groceries and made ten sack lunches. They took them to a park in downtown Baltimore where the homeless gathered.

"We gave away four lunches," [recalls the father], "then Anthony pointed out a group of men. He had been afraid to get out of the van . . . [but] he said to Tony, 'If you take my hand, Dad, I think I can give these lunches to them.' These men were so grateful. They were trying to split a piece of gum between them."

It was obviously more than a one-time project. Baltimore has about twenty-seven hundred homeless, and its soup kitchens can feed only about fifteen hundred. The Franquellis went back every week with more lunches, until they were giving away a hundred a week and stretching the family budget so far that Sister Franquelli even sold some jewelry to help buy the food. Then other members of the ward got involved, a newspaper article resulted in some contributions from the community, and merchants began to donate bread and other items. Several other families also started doing lunches for a family project. The Franquellis make between five hundred and seven hundred lunches each Saturday in their two-car garage with the help of missionaries, single members, and other workers. They deliver them on Sunday and take along about three hundred extra sandwiches.

Sister Franquelli, who suffers from a terminal liver disease, says, "Doing this work brings one of the greatest spiritual feelings we've ever had in our lives. . . . There have been times when we have driven back from Baltimore when we couldn't talk." Brother Franquelli says that the most important thing is learning to give unconditionally. "When you give unconditionally, it doesn't make a difference who you give to. You have to . . . give without putting conditions on the giving." ("Feeding Homeless Sparks Spirit of Service, Unity," *Church News*, 23 May 1992, pp. 5–6.)

Why do they do it? Can you feel their joy and their desire to serve? Where does it come from, if not from Christ?

CONCLUSION

For many of us, the Spirit of Christ is a familiar and a

beloved Spirit. We feel it often in our home. It stirs our heart as we kneel in prayer. We feel it accompanying us as we exert ourselves in acts of service for others. For some of us, perhaps this Spirit is not so familiar. When we talk about being "rooted and grounded in love," this tenderness of heart, this feeling of connectedness to others—this feeling is what we mean. Keeping a balance in our life means having deep roots. It is not a matter of piling our plate high with beans, juggling scripture study and jogging, squeezing in banana bread for the sisters we visit teach, and choosing a present for a baby shower—all in the same crowded day. Those things will happen—I promise you they will happen—and they will happen without worry and without cramming and juggling.

Our hands will find deeds of kindness to do just as words of kindness will spring to our lips before we even know that we are searching for them, because the roots of our relationship with Christ will keep that nourishing flow coming. It is the water of life, springing up in us, refreshing us, cleansing us, anointing us—and spilling over through us to anoint and bless others.

I feel to promise with the prophet Isaiah: "And the Lord shall guide thee continually, and satisfy thy soul in drought, and make fat thy bones: and thou shalt be like a watered garden, and like a spring of water, whose waters fail not." (Isaiah 58:11.) That is the Lord's blessing. It will be fulfilled.

CHAPTER 6

Following Him

Few invitations come to us with such warmth and simultaneously with such challenge as this invitation to follow our Savior:

> And [Jesus] said to them all, If any [of you] will come after me, . . . deny [your]self, and take [your] cross daily, and follow me.
>
> For whosoever will save [your] life shall lose it: but whosoever will lose [your] life for my sake, the same shall save it. (Luke 9:23–24)

Let me share with you four principles of following the Savior that I hope will paint a bigger picture in our minds of what it all means.

First, we can follow the Savior in establishing a personal relationship with our Father in Heaven.

Second, we can follow the Savior in serving.

Third, we can follow the Savior in forgiving others.

Fourth, we can follow the Savior in reaching across barriers.

A FIRSTHAND RELATIONSHIP

To set the theme for the first principle, think of the beloved hymn, "God Loved Us, So He Sent His Son" (*Hymns* [Salt

Lake City: The Church of Jesus Christ of Latter-day Saints, 1985], no. 187):

> *God loved us, so he sent his Son,*
> *Christ Jesus, the atoning One,*
> *To show us by the path he trod*
> *The one and only way to God.*
>
> *He came as man, though Son of God,*
> *And bowed himself beneath the rod.*
> *He died in holy innocence,*
> *A broken law to recompense.*
>
> *Oh, love effulgent, love divine!*
> *What debt of gratitude is mine,*
> *That in his off'ring I have part*
> *And hold a place within his heart.*

I particularly love the last line that reminds all of us that we, too, "hold a place within his heart." When I think about the many things the Savior did and said, the way he led his life and the willingness he had to offer up that perfect life for us, I wonder how he could do it. And I think that he could do it because he carried in his heart the shining image of his Father's perfect love for him.

Jesus said, "I and my Father are one." (John 10:30.) To me that means that whenever the Savior had to make a decision, he consistently and continually referred that decision to the image in his heart. He asked himself, "Uh oh. Here come some self-righteous men dragging a woman taken in adultery. What would my Father do? What would he say to the men? What would he say to the woman?"

What Jesus actually did was something that seems fairly mystifying on the face of it. He said nothing. He stooped and wrote something in the dust and then said one sentence that wasn't really addressed to anyone in particular and that didn't seem to have much to do with the correct and legally prescribed punishment for an adulterous woman. He said, "He that is without sin among you, let him first cast a stone at her." Stung by their own guilty consciences, those men who had been ready to kill this woman melted away. Then Jesus asked the woman where her accusers were. When she pointed out the obvious—that they had gone—he said kindly, "Neither do I condemn thee: go, and sin no more." (John 8:7–11.) That turned out to be exactly the right thing to do.

When Jesus saw Zacchaeus in the tree, I think he asked himself what his Father would do—walk on by? scold him? tell him to come down and be preached to? All of those were logical and reasonable things to do. Instead, he did something mystifying and puzzling. He told Zacchaeus to come down— that he was inviting himself and his apostles to Zacchaeus' house for dinner that day. Zacchaeus had just been ignored by a whole crowd of taller people; and he'd probably, as a tax collector, been scolded by experts before. Neither one of those things would have done much good. But to be invited to dinner—even if he was supplying the house and the dinner— now that was such a bizarre and unusual thing that Zacchaeus didn't even hesitate! (See Luke 19:2–6.) But once again, it turned out to be exactly the right thing to do.

I'm suggesting that Jesus always did the right thing because he carried in his heart the divine image of his Father in Heaven. He could not say or do things that did not fit that image. That's what we need, a divine image so clear and powerful that we can recognize it and tell if our actions are matching it. Jesus said, "My sheep hear my voice." (John 10:27.) We, too, can hear and recognize the voice of the Savior.

Each one of us needs a firsthand relationship with the Savior—a primary relationship, not a secondary one. The testimonies that others have of Jesus are powerful and strengthening, but if we rely on them instead of developing our own relationship, we will be spiritually weak. The manuals and the *Ensign* and other commentaries and sermons and essays are meaningful and perceptive; but if we read only them and don't study the scriptures for ourselves, we will have only a secondhand relationship with the scriptures. The prayers of others can be uplifting and spiritual, but if we don't pray our own prayers, we will be distant from the Savior.

Let's follow the Savior in establishing a firsthand relationship with our Father in Heaven, a relationship so strong that it will fill our hearts so that we can, without confusion, follow him by following our hearts. "Draw near unto me," the Lord says, "and I will draw near unto you; seek me diligently and ye shall find me." (D&C 88:63.) I know this promise is true because he has drawn near to me and guided me as I have diligently sought his companionship.

SERVICE

To express the theme of service, consider the beautiful hymn "Lord, I Would Follow Thee" (*Hymns*, no. 220):

> *Savior, may I learn to love thee,*
> *Walk the path that thou hast shown,*
> *Pause to help and lift another,*

Finding strength beyond my own.
Savior, may I learn to love thee—
Lord, I would follow thee.

Who am I to judge another?
When I walk imperfectly?
In the quiet heart is hidden
Sorrow that the eye can't see.
Who am I to judge another—
Lord, I would follow thee.

I would be [another's] keeper;
I would learn the healer's art.
To the wounded and the weary
I would show a gentle heart.
I would be [another's] keeper—
Lord, I would follow thee.

Savior, may I love [another]
As I know thou lovest me,
Find in thee my strength, my beacon,
For thy servant I would be.
Savior, may I love [another]—
Lord, I would follow thee.

All over the Church during 1992, Relief Society sisters celebrated the sesquicentennial with a wonderful year of service, particularly community service. The Relief Society general offices were flooded with reports, each one more inspiring than the one before. Service is the signature of the Relief Society, and it's the signature of the Savior. As King Benjamin pointed out, "When ye are in the service of your fellow beings ye are only in the service of your God." (Mosiah 2:17.) And as Jesus promised, "Inasmuch as ye have done it unto one of the least of these . . . , ye have done it unto me." (Matthew 25:40.)

We know that service is indispensable for bringing us close to the Savior and letting us feel his Spirit. In nothing do we resemble the Savior more than in serving others. So in nothing should we feel greater love and joy than in service.

But I'm aware, from my discussions with many women, that service can sometimes be perceived as a burden, an obligation, something to get through, something that we drag along and are dragged down by. What if the joy isn't there? What then? Well, that's the point I want to focus on right now. If the joy is gone from service, we often just feel guilty. We blame ourselves for having a bad attitude. We redouble our efforts. We make longer lists. We take on more projects. We have worse experiences. We reproach ourselves more. We work more anxiously. And the joy gets farther away.

Service may be a duty and a responsibility, but it is also voluntary, not compulsory. If your service is starting to feel like a job, then you need to change things to get the joy back. I think that often the problem is that we are no longer choosing. *We* are not seeing needs. Someone else is. And *we* are not responding to the need of an individual whose need we see. We're just responding to an assignment instead of choosing to help a brother or sister. Guilt-sponsored service may get some necessary jobs done, but I'm not sure it gets many joy-filled jobs done.

I think that the solution is to remember the principle of agency. Agency allows us to say no, which is difficult for many of us to do, as well as yes. Otherwise our yes doesn't mean very much. That wonderful Japanese word *kigatsuku* means having an inner spirit to see good and do it voluntarily. It's easier to say yes, I think, if we're responding to the needs of a widow whose daughter is on a mission instead of Service Project 14B. It's easier to feel the joy of service if we have in our awareness a consciousness of the Savior's own great joy in serving others.

My eldest grandson, Matthew, is a wonderful boy, very helpful and alert. Ed and I were visiting for Thanksgiving of 1991 when Matthew was four, and Ed was helping our son Bob finish the basement. Whenever they sawed boards, they would make a mess with the sawdust on the floor, so in every break, Ed would reach for the broom. When Matthew saw him sweeping, he'd run and get the dustpan without being told and hold it for him. Then Ed would say, "Matthew, you are being a *kigatsuku* boy. You're helping Bapa and Daddy a lot. Thank you so much!" Matthew helped in every way he could all day long.

Then, just when they were cleaning up for supper at five o'clock, Ed started sweeping one more time, but Matthew didn't bring the dustpan. Ed looked around and saw Matthew sitting on the steps just looking at the scene. "Matthew," he called, "I'm sweeping."

Matthew said, "I'm sick and tired of this. I don't care if you get the broom, Bapa. I'm not getting the dustpan."

Ed and Bob looked at each other, laughed, and finished the cleanup by themselves. The next morning, Matthew was on the job with them bright and early again. What if they'd scolded him? What if Bob had been embarrassed and thought Matthew was being rude to his grandfather? What if they'd forced him to serve? I wonder how he would have felt about helping the next morning. But because he was free to choose, he chose to serve again, and he felt good about it.

You know what your resources and your circumstances are. There come times in every life when there's just nothing left to give. King Benjamin gave us a model to follow in such times: "I would that ye say in your hearts that: I give not because I have not, but if I had I would give." (Mosiah 4:24.)

I don't want you to misunderstand me. Some reasons for saying no are not good reasons. For example, fear. We sometimes want to say no to a calling or an assignment out of fear, because we're afraid we can't do it right. When we have to struggle with fear, let's pray for more faith. The apostle Paul said, "I can do all things through Christ which strengtheneth me." (Philippians 4:13.)

A second reason why we sometimes want to say no is out of selfishness. When we have to struggle with selfishness, let's pray for more charity, the pure love of Christ. But if we come to a season in our lives when King Benjamin's counsel applies to us, let's pray to know clearly our limits and our priorities. We have the same commitment to say both of those simple words, yes and no, but we must do it wisely and responsibly.

Let me tell you one more story about my grandson. For Thanksgiving dinner, I was making chocolate turkeys with malt balls and chocolate stars and frosting lines for the heads and wings. Matthew scrambled up to the table and exclaimed, "I can do that, Nana!"

I said, "Great! Here you go."

He tried it all the way through, and it turned out to be

pretty complicated for his little fingers, so he said, "I think you'd better do this, Nana. But I can do *this* part." He could place the malt balls where they needed to go. And he stayed with me until we finished the whole project, placing the malt balls for the feet of each turkey.

He felt good about trying everything, but he knew what he could do and what he couldn't do. That's a lot of wisdom for a little boy. Do we know ourselves that well? We are instructed that "it is not requisite that [we] should run faster than [we have] strength." (Mosiah 4:27.) Let's look at our own circumstances, appraise our own strength, get in touch with our desires. Let's do what we can do; and when we do, there's joy in our job. Let's use our own agency. Let's choose freely and wisely, and do the best we can, if it is only to put the feet on the body of the turkey.

And finally, let's remember that all kinds of service are acceptable to the Lord. We may think that service is getting out there and collecting funds for a children's orthopedic unit or a homeless shelter. Sometimes it is. But sometimes it's writing out the check for the volunteer who comes canvassing and saying to her sincerely, "Thank you so much for giving your time to do this. I hope that someday I can do the same thing." Choose wisely, so that the things of greatest value during your particular season have the highest priority. That way, our service stays a joy, not a job.

We don't need to compare ourselves to anyone else. The service we can offer will always stretch us a little beyond our own boundaries, but what we can offer is okay even if it's just a few resources, just a few minutes. Jesus healed a blind man in a few seconds with spit and mud. We don't have to measure up to somebody else's checklist of perfection. The Lord loves and appreciates us, just the way we are. We can follow the Savior in serving others. Jesus told the Nephites: "Verily, verily, I say unto you, this is my gospel; . . . the works which ye have seen me do that shall ye also do." (3 Nephi 27:21.) Now that's an uncomplicated definition of the gospel that I can manage with no confusion.

The first two concepts seem to go together, don't they? First, we can have a primary, personal, firsthand relationship with our Heavenly Father and learn to carry the image of the Savior in our hearts. Second, service then becomes a joy because we will want to follow Christ in serving each other. It makes it easier when we do things for the right reasons and overlook the difficulties and obstacles that are part of mortality.

FORGIVENESS

To set the theme for the topic of forgiveness, think of that lovely sailor's hymn for men's chorus (*Hymns*, no. 335), "Brightly Beams Our Father's Mercy":

> *Brightly beams our Father's mercy*
> *From his lighthouse evermore,*
> *But to us he gives the keeping*
> *Of the lights along the shore.*
>
> *Chorus:*
> *Let the lower lights be burning;*
> *Send a gleam across the wave.*
> *Some poor fainting, struggling seaman*
> *You may rescue, you may save.*

Dark the night of sin has settled;
Loud the angry billows roar.
Eager eyes are watching, longing,
For the lights along the shore.

Trim your feeble lamp, my [sister],
Some poor sailor, tempest-tossed,
Trying now to make the harbor,
In the darkness may be lost.

This hymn was a favorite of my husband, Ed. He loved to sing, and he loved the harmony in this song, but he also loved the feeling that there was a shore and a light in what sometimes felt like a huge ocean of indifference and even hatred. When you grow up on an island, you became very sensitive to the ocean and its moods, aware that you can't really trust it, and yet you are dependent upon it and even more dependent on those who trim their feeble lamps.

Ed knew a lot about forgiveness. He was a member of the 442d Division, a unit of Japanese-American soldiers that fought in Europe during World War II. Most of them were from Hawaii. It had the highest rate of casualties and the highest rate of decorations of any unit on the Allied side, and that kind of tells the whole story right there. Ed was so severely wounded in France that it took him a year to recuperate.

Many of the men who were his comrades in arms had fathers and uncles who were in American internment camps, just because they were of Japanese ancestry. Ed and many of the other soldiers had been in the ROTC unit at the University of Hawaii. When war was declared, they were all mobilized; but within a few weeks, the Japanese ROTC members were discharged—just for being Japanese. They pleaded for a chance to serve their country, and when the 442d Division was organized to fight in Europe, they competed with each other to join up. They did not let bitterness consume them. They asked only for a chance. When we came to Utah, we had a hard time finding a place to live or to build a house because we were Japanese. One insurance company wouldn't insure our car. Some people made unkind remarks on the street. I never saw Ed lose his temper or even his patience. He just forgave and stayed focused on the gospel.

Ed understood the power of forgiveness in overcoming the destructive power of hatred and resentment, and when the fifty-year anniversaries of World War II events were observed, he was keenly interested and deeply moved. I remember how touched he was at the account of an earlier story of reconciliation and forgiveness:

> Captain Ben W. Blee, retired from the U.S. Navy, wrote about the reunion in Wilmington, North Carolina, aboard the retired battleship *USS North Carolina*, of a group of American survivors and four former crew members of a Japanese submarine, the IJN I-19. They had met in the battle of the South Pacific known as Torpedo Junction. The IJN I-19 had torpedoed and sunk an aircraft carrier and a warship and had disabled the *North Carolina*. Captain Blee explains the terrible complexity of the gesture of peace they were trying to make:
>
> "Untold hundreds, perhaps thousands, of Japanese were killed by the *North Carolina's* guns. Could we, or they, in good conscience make friends with some of the very men who had done the killing?"

Captain Blee acknowledged that those feelings were strong and real and then concluded:

"To go to our graves still seething with hatred would serve no good purpose. Our lifelong obligation to the dead will be far better honored if we do what we can to build harmony and goodwill in the world. . . . It is not enough for former enemies merely to decide in the privacy of their own minds that they no longer hate or distrust each other. To give that decision any real meaning, we believed we had to meet and express our feelings man to man."

As the four Japanese submariners walked forward along the deck, more than a hundred American veterans of the war in the Pacific saluted them and applauded warmly. Facing the port bow of the old battleship, the two groups held a joint memorial service and exchanged identical commemorative plaques in both languages that read: "Having endured the perils of World War II as mortal enemies, we now offer to each other the hand of friendship, fervently sharing the hope that the sacrifices made in that war will never be forgotten or repeated."

One of the four Japanese former submarine crew members of the IJN I-19, Quartermaster Rishichi Sugiyama, said that the invitation was "almost incomprehensible by Japanese standards." Torpedoman Shichiro Tange said, "It gave me the most exalted experience of my life to participate in the solemn joint memorial service. . . . If only all people in the world can proceed hand in hand with courage and determination to maintain peace in the world after the pattern set by this reunion! We have a solemn obligation to convey this feeling to our descendants."

Another memorial service held on Iwo Jima commemorated the battle in which twenty thousand Japanese soldiers and seven thousand U.S. Marines died. "They were reconciled through a worship service, and a memorial has been constructed and dedicated as a testimony of that reconciliation." (Duane E. Couey, "Peace and Reconciliation," *Saints Herald*, May 1991, pp. 13–14.)

I have used the example of war partly because of Ed's song and partly because of my own feelings. Perhaps that is an overdramatic example. Think of the daily little injuries, the unintentional snub, the thoughtless remark, the unjust comparison, the swift stereotype—all of the ways in which we injure and harm other human beings. All of them require forgiveness. The Savior warned the Latter-day Saints through Joseph Smith:

> My disciples, in days of old, sought occasion against one another and forgave not one another in their hearts; and for this evil they were afflicted and sorely chastened.
>
> Wherefore, I say unto you, that ye ought to forgive one another; for [she] that forgiveth not [her sister her] trespasses standeth condemned before the Lord; for there remaineth in [her] the greater sin.
>
> I, the Lord, will forgive whom I will forgive, but of you it is required to forgive all. . . .
>
> And ye ought to say in your hearts—let God judge between me and thee, and reward thee according to thy deeds. (D&C 64:8–11)

The commandment to forgive is universal. Ultimately we both must and can forgive all who have trespassed against us, but I do not suggest that forgiveness is always quick or easy. Forgiveness is a change of heart, and sometimes a great deal of healing must take place before forgiveness can occur.

I think we have all become more aware of that requirement as the terrible dynamic of sexual abuse is being studied and discussed more widely in the Church. I hope you have had a chance to read the anonymous article in the *Ensign* in January 1992 in which a sister talks about being sexually abused by her active Latter-day Saint father and how, because of the abuse, she learned, she said, to "turn off my feelings . . . to completely separate my mind from my body. . . . I am so expert at distracting myself from the realities of the present that, until a short time ago, I was unaware that I was even doing it." She didn't trust her father. She didn't trust God. She never felt safe or loved until she recognized the anger she felt at her father for abusing her, at her mother for not protecting her, at the Church for believing her father, at God for letting it happen, at herself for being a victim. Those were very painful feelings; but when she let herself feel the "anger, the hurt, and the rejection," then she could also start to feel "God's pure love for [her]." She discovered new courage, new compassion for others. She writes:

> One of the most difficult yet most rewarding aspects of this entire experience has been my quest to reach a point where I could forgive my father. In the early stages of my grief, the Holy Ghost revealed to me over and over that God does indeed love me. I began to pray more often and more earnestly. I read more scriptures and sought comfort, hope, and answers. I knew I couldn't forgive my father on my own, so I asked God to help me. And he has.
>
> I have realized that my father's repentance is his job, not mine. I'm not sure Dad understands how much he has hurt his children and others. When the day comes that he does, I know he will truly mourn. Should the day come that he approaches the Father with a broken heart and a contrite spirit, I do know this: Like the father of the prodigal son, God will open his arms and welcome him home. And I, like

the brother in the story, have learned to open my heart and love again. ("A Refuge for the Oppressed," *Ensign,* Jan. 1992, pp. 62–64)

There are two messages in this sister's story for me: the first is that forgiveness of even the most grievous injuries is possible; the second is that, in such circumstances as sexual abuse, forgiveness can take a long time. Don't let other people set timetables for you or tell you that you've finished some spiritual business if you yourself know that there is more work to be done.

Consider this wonderful one-sentence letter from a child to God: "Dear God, I am doing the best I can. Frank." (*Children's Letters to God,* comp. Eric Marshall and Stuart Hample, enl. ed. [New York: Pocket Books, 1975], n. p.)

That's all God wants—progress toward the goal. No one who has felt the sweetness of being forgiven or of forgiving another can possibly want to cling to feelings of resentment one second longer than absolutely necessary, but forgiveness *is* a gift. It comes to us through the grace of Christ. And speaking the words of forgiveness before our hearts have changed, even if we most desperately want the words to be true, may only postpone the actual gift itself. But I can assure you, in time, with continued faithfulness and through the grace of Christ, the gift of forgiveness will surely come.

REACHING ACROSS BARRIERS

Now let's consider how we can follow the Savior by reaching across barriers of diversity that seem to separate us from each other. Unity is a wonderful principle of the gospel. The Savior told the Latter-day Saints, "I say unto you, be one; and if ye are not one ye are not mine." (D&C 38:27.) The psalmist rejoiced, "Behold, how good and how pleasant it is for brethren to dwell together in unity!" (Psalm 133:1.)

The apostle Paul wrote to the Ephesians:

> There is one body, and one Spirit, even as ye are called in one hope of your calling;
>
> One Lord, one faith, one baptism,
>
> One God and Father of all, who is above all, and through all, and in you all. (Ephesians 4:4–6)

Yes, unity is important in the Church. But sometimes we misread these strong messages for unity as instructions to look alike, talk alike, dress alike, think alike, have the same number of children, keep house a certain way, have prayers at certain times, serve green Jell-O for certain meals, or have plastic grapes in the living room. You get the point. Complete conformity in our personalities and styles of living is not the same thing as unity of spirit, unity of testimony, and unity of faith in the Savior.

Unity in the Church grows from a few great master principles: our eternal identity as children of our Heavenly Parents, our eternal and inescapable right and responsibility to exercise agency, the divine mission of the Lord Jesus Christ, the prophetic calling of Joseph Smith and his successors down to our current prophet, the centrality of the scriptures, and our baptismal commitment to live together as Christians, bound together by our understanding of the gospel and by our loving service to each other. But when it comes to practices— how we learn, how we pray to the Father, how we apply the teachings of the prophets, what shape our service takes—

in all of these, there is great room for individuality. Let's acknowledge it and rejoice in it.

Here's one of my favorite proverbs: "If both of us think alike, one of us is not necessary." Well, all of us *are* necessary. We all think different thoughts, have different perceptions, enjoy different opinions, and rejoice in our diversity. Diversity means uniqueness and difference. It is a cause for celebration within our Church membership. Diversity is not a danger to be stamped out, a broken thing to be fixed, or a sin to be repented of. We'll be stronger, healthier, more interesting, and more capable when we learn to enjoy differences instead of feeling frightened about them or angry because of them.

Now, with that as an introduction, think of a hymn that celebrates both diversity and unity. It is the lovely hymn of St. Francis of Assisi that calls on all of the diverse creations of God to praise him and show forth his glory (*Hymns*, no. 62):

> *All creatures of our God and King,*
> *Lift up your voice and with us sing,*
> *Alleluia! Alleluia!*
> *Thou burning sun with golden beam,*
> *Thou silver moon with softer gleam,*
> *Alleluia! Alleluia!*
> *Alleluia! Oh, praise him! Alleluia!*
>
> *Thou rushing wind that art so strong,*
> *Ye clouds that sail in heav'n along,*
> *Alleluia! Alleluia!*
> *Thou rising morn, in praise rejoice;*
> *Ye light of evening, find a voice,*

Alleluia! Alleluia!
Alleluia! Oh, praise him! Alleluia!

Thou flowing water, pure and clear,
Make music for thy Lord to hear,
Alleluia! Alleluia!
Thou fire so masterful and bright,
That gives to [us] both warmth and light,
Alleluia! Alleluia!
Alleluia! Oh, praise him! Alleluia!

Dear Mother Earth, who day by day
Unfoldest blessings on our way,
Alleluia! Alleluia!
The flow'rs and fruit that in thee grow,
Let them his glory also show,
Alleluia! Alleluia!
Alleluia! Oh, praise him! Alleluia!

We all have different personalities, but we can all unite our voices in singing praises to God using the English translation of the words of an Italian saint in the Catholic church. There is room in the world for all of us. There is room in God's love for all of us, and there is room in the Church for all of us.

Sometimes we have what I call the Too Syndrome. We feel that there are some people we can't really extend full acceptance to because they are too something—too old, too young, too liberal, too conservative, too rich, too poor, too educated, too uneducated, too rigid in religious observances, too lax. In the parable of the good Samaritan, if the traveler who fell among thieves was like other Jews of his time, he felt that Samaritans were too ethnically impure to worship in the temple; I don't think he felt that the wine and the oil poured on his wounds were too Samaritan, do you?

I feel strongly about this principle of reaching past barriers because I'm so grateful for all the people in my life who have not been afflicted with the Too Syndrome. I'm grateful to the missionary who did not think that I was too Buddhist to learn about Jesus. I'm grateful to the elder who did not think that fifteen was too young to be baptized. I'm grateful to Ed for not thinking that I was too Mormon to marry into his Congregationalist family and who did not think that his family ties were too strong to keep him from being baptized himself when he gained a testimony of the truthfulness of the gospel. I'm grateful to Florence Jacobsen, who did not think I was too Japanese to be on the YWMIA general board in 1961. I'm grateful to the bishop who did not think that as a school principal I was too busy to be a Relief Society president. I was not too anything for those people. I was enough.

We, too, can follow the Savior by reaching beyond diverse circumstances that seem to separate us from other members of the Church and other people in our community.

CONCLUSION

We've talked about following the Savior in establishing a personal relationship with our Father in Heaven, in serving, in forgiving others, and in reaching across the barriers of diversity that separate us from our brothers and sisters.

If we had been able literally to follow Jesus, tagging along at his elbow, as it were, during his mortal ministry, there are parts of it that would have been wonderful and other parts that would have been very trying. We would have grown hot, hungry, dusty, and thirsty. We would have been jostled by crowds and had to rely on the hospitality of others for food and shelter. We would sometimes have been confused by the teachings of Jesus and struggled to understand why he did some of the things he did and what he meant by some of the things he said.

There would also have been moments of love that touched us to the very heart and transformed our souls. There would have come moments of transcendent awareness when we knew that we stood in the presence of the very God foretold by Moses, Isaiah, and Jeremiah. We would have seen ourselves as Jesus saw us—limited and frustratingly inadequate but also infinitely precious, unendingly worthy of his love. We would never have wanted to be anywhere other than where we were. We would never have imagined a love stronger and deeper than the love that filled us for Jesus.

We would also have understood, as the disciples did, that the way of Jesus led not only to the mount of penetrating sermons, to the hillsides where miracles of loaves and fishes occurred, to the quiet rooms of healing and blessing but also to the garden, the cross, and the tomb. The way of the disciple is that same path. The confusion of the disciples as they groped toward a testimony of the Savior as the Son of God finally yielded to the witness of the Spirit that he was in very deed the literal Son of God. Once possessing that understanding, think of their bewilderment and anguish at seeing him, the Lord of all creation, hanging on the cross, crucified by the very people he had come to save. And yet, even this bewilderment gave way to their joyous witness of his glorious resurrection.

We have taken upon ourselves the name of Jesus and the way of the disciple. Our way will also lead to gardens of anguished prayer, to crosses, to tombs. At those times, we, like the apostles, must endure in faith and love. We must endure despite our pain, *with* our pain, in the depths of our pain, until the moment of the resurrection in us when we understand the greater purpose in the cross and the tomb. I testify to you that those moments of understanding and acceptance will come.

The loss of my beloved husband is the hardest thing that has ever happened to me. I am a triple cancer survivor. I have been near death three times from other causes. Those were testing times. Sometimes I thought I had been tested to the point of breaking. But none of them compares with the testing following Ed's death. There have been times when I literally could not turn the doorknob and leave the house without praying for strength and imploring the Lord for his Spirit to accompany me as I went out to perform my duties. All of us must face death—our own deaths and the deaths of loved ones. I feel that I am learning something about the way of the disciple that leads through the valley of the shadow of death, but even there—*even there*—I know I am following the Savior, and I can feel his hand upholding me and his voice promising me, "I will never leave thee, nor forsake thee." (Hebrews 13:5.)

May we all follow the Savior, even though the disciple's path is stony and shadowed. May we feel the presence of the Savior with us on that path, and may we sustain and support one another as we walk together. I pray upon us the blessing that the apostle Paul invoked upon the Thessalonian Saints as they walked their own disciple's path:

The Lord make you to increase and abound in love one toward another, and toward all . . .

To the end [that] he may stablish your hearts unblameable in holiness before God, even our Father, at the coming of our Lord Jesus Christ with all his saints. (1 Thessalonians 3:12–13)

May we be among their joyous number!

PART 3

The Way of the Christian

CHAPTER 7

The Way of the Christian

What does it mean to follow the way of the Christian? And what could be more appropriate than that those who have taken upon themselves the name of Christ at the waters of baptism should reflect together on what it means to follow our Savior?

I'd like to share with you two ways of following the Savior, ways that we can all follow as we come unto Christ: first, have a primary relationship with the Savior; and second, serve others with love, not judgment. Those are prime characteristics of the way of the Christian.

HAVE A PRIMARY RELATIONSHIP WITH THE SAVIOR

We all need to have a primary relationship with the Savior—a firsthand relationship, not a secondhand or hand-me-down relationship from our parents or our teachers. We need a personal, intimate relationship, one that is based on our own experiences with the Savior, our own answered prayers, our own knowledge of what the Spirit feels like, our own obedience to its guidance, our own knowledge that Christ atoned for us. A secondhand relationship is based on knowing people who know the Savior and believing their testimony. I don't want to suggest that there is anything wrong with doing so in part. The scriptures tell us:

> To some it is given by the Holy Ghost to know that Jesus Christ is the Son of God, and that he was crucified for the sins of the world.
>
> To others it is given to believe on their words, that they also might have eternal life if they continue faithful. (D&C 46:13–14)

But the scriptures also promise:

> Verily, thus saith the Lord: It shall come to pass that every soul who forsaketh his sins and cometh unto me, and calleth on my name, and obeyeth my voice, and keepeth my commandments, shall see my face and know that I am;
>
> And that I am the true light that lighteth every man that cometh into the world. (D&C 93:1–2)

To me, this passage means that the spiritual gift of believing on the testimony of others is meant to lead us to the greater gift of receiving a direct and personal knowledge of the Savior. My husband, Ed, had this personal knowledge from the time he was a child. I grew up in a Buddhist home and discovered Christianity as part of the intriguing but puzzling world of the *haoles* who ran our plantation. Ed was raised a Congregationalist and had a great love for the Savior from the time he was a little boy. It was this great love that I recognized in him when we met at the University of Hawaii as students and began dating. Many people warned me against getting too serious about Ed, because he wasn't a Mormon and they were afraid that I would become inactive. But I recognized in Ed a purity of heart and a thirst for goodness that whispered to me that he would accept greater truth when he recognized it. With that faith, I took the risk of marrying him; he was baptized ten months after our wedding. The gospel added to the faith and love he already had for Jesus, building on the foundation established in him during his youth.

I want to share some experiences that show the quality of Ed's faith, stories that Ed prepared just two weeks before his death to share with the Lambda Delta Sigma unit in Salt Lake City when he introduced me as their speaker. He told them about four miracles in our family, not because our family is uniquely special but because he wanted to testify to those young women that each one is equally precious to her Heavenly Father. I already knew of Ed's love and support, but his expressing those feelings in writing just a few days before his death made them doubly precious to me. I speak of these four miracles in Ed's own words as examples of his faith:

> When Chieko was in labor at the birth of our second son, she felt her spirit drifting upwards out of her body. She struggled against the feeling, fighting to get back to deliver the baby. I was in the waiting room and felt the sudden urgent need to pray. The only private room I could find was a tiny toilet off the hallway. I went in, closed the lid, knelt down, and prayed humbly for my wife. The Lord preserved her.
>
> The second time, we came home from work and Chieko complained of a temperature and a pain in her arm. We called our family doctor who told her to take two aspirins and call him in the morning. By midnight, she was in great pain. I was a social worker at the V.A. Hospital and called my friend, Dr. Howard Latimer. When I described the symptoms, he asked, "Can you see a blue line running up her arm to the armpit?" I checked. There was the line. "It's

staph infection," he said. "I'll be right there." He came at once, started antibiotics on an IV, and stayed with me all night. "If you'd waited," he told us, "Chieko would have been dead by morning."

The third time, we were in Denver. For some reason, I had had the car running in the garage next to the kitchen. When I came into the kitchen, I saw Chieko slumped at the table over her schoolwork. I knew immediately that she had been poisoned by the carbon monoxide fumes. Our son Bob and I picked her up, took her outside, draped her arm over my shoulder, and walked her up and down until the oxygen revived her, and then took her to the hospital. Heavenly Father preserved her life a third time.

A few months later, she discovered a lump in her breast. Three days later, she was admitted to the hospital and we signed the consent forms for a mastectomy to be performed if the biopsy proved to be malignant. It was, but she has outlived her doctor. For the fourth time, Heavenly Father preserved her life.

Ed told these stories to make the point that my life had been spared for a purpose. I tell them to you to make the point that Ed was a man of God whose faith in our Heavenly Father and Jesus Christ was absolute. He saw the hand of God in these experiences because he lived close to the Spirit.

Prayers are not little set speeches that we deliver at stated times during the day or rituals for opening and closing meetings. Think of prayer as a sustained, ongoing conversation that you have with God during the whole day. Mother Teresa tells the Sisters of Charity who work with her among the poor in Calcutta:

Love to pray—feel often during the day the need for prayer, and take [the] trouble to pray. Prayer enlarges the

heart until it is capable of containing God's gift
Ask and seek, and your heart will grow b
receive him and keep him as your own.
receive in silent prayer, the more we ca
life. We need silence to be able to touch
thing is not what we say, but what
through us. All our words will be us
from within—words which do not
increase the darkness. (Malcolm
Beautiful for God: Mother Teresa
Walker and Co./Phoenix Press,
pp. 60–61)

If your relationship with the L
like it to be, I encourage you to spend in
prayer. Sometimes we think that we must meet a
specifications before we're worthy to approach him. Or sometimes we think that we must withdraw completely from our
daily activities to meet him. Perhaps both of these things are
partially true in some circumstances, but I testify to you that
he is already with us in those daily circumstances and
he stands beside us as we anxiously check off good deeds on
our endless lists, patiently waiting for us to notice him. He
doesn't call us away from our daily activities; he asks simply
that we let him be with us as we carry them out—including
the carpooling, the housecleaning, the parent-teacher conferences, the meetings at work, and the meetings at church.
Prayer is an endlessly refreshing and delightful dialogue that
can be carried on, even without words, between the heart in
tune and the Spirit of the Lord.

So my first point is, Follow the way of the Christian by following the way of prayer.

SERVE WITH LOVE

My second point is that as Christians we should serve with love, not judgment. Judging others and labeling their motives and their behavior puts an obstacle in the paths that we try to follow as Christians. It always hurts and grieves me when members of the Church condemn people who don't keep the Word of Wisdom and make them feel that they'll be welcome at church just as soon as they stop smoking. Where will they get the strength to change if they feel condemned until they become perfect?

I am so grateful for the commandment of the Savior, "Judge not, that ye be not judged." (Matthew 7:1.) Some of our leaders in the Church—our bishops and stake presidents—are called to be judges. It is a heavy burden they bear, and I pray for them to bear it righteously. But I am glad not to have that responsibility. I am glad that I can focus on other parts of the gospel, especially just loving others. We can be free of the burden of judging others' motives or achievements, how they raise their children, or how well they do their church jobs. And we can be especially free of that burden in relation to ourselves.

We must stop judging ourselves and get on with the Christian business of loving and forgiving ourselves, along with loving others.

Sister Ida Smith of Brigham Young University put this concept into a wonderful perspective:

> No two of us are alike. We have not had identical backgrounds, our current experiences vary enormously, our timetables are not the same. It is important that we not compare ourselves with others, which often causes us to see

ourselves in a negative light. Also, we must constantly guard against the temptation to assume that where there is a difference, there must also automatically be a defect. Too often we not only berate ourselves, but each other as well, saying, "If you were really a righteous woman, you would/ wouldn't be doing what you're doing!" If we are honestly doing what we feel we must do for ourselves and our loved ones, and are doing so because that is our choice, ratified by the Spirit, we have the right to feel good about ourselves and to be free of feelings of guilt. There is a world of difference between *being* guilty and *feeling* guilty, and women are far too prone to allow themselves to feel guilty when they're not living up to someone else's expectations of what they should or should not be doing. ("LDS Women: At Home and Beyond," in *As Women of Faith: Talks Selected from the BYU Women's Conferences,* ed. Mary E. Stovall and Carol Cornwall Madsen [Salt Lake City: Deseret Book, 1991], p. 214)

Remember that the gospel is good news—the good news that our Heavenly Father and Jesus loved us so much that Jesus came among us to show us how to live and to die for us. The way of the Christian involves drawing near to him in ongoing, loving prayer, in not checking the flow of the Spirit by judging others, and by letting the sunshine into our own lives by not judging ourselves harshly.

When we set aside the burden of judgment, then our hands and hearts are free to serve others with joy. Such service is truly the way of the Christian.

Ed never worried about finding someone to serve and he never worried about the service itself. Whoever Ed was with had his undivided interest—a teenager in the foyer on the way to sacrament meeting who needed a warm smile and a handshake, a stranger sitting next to him at a political rally with a few minutes to pass before it started, a car stranded by the side of the road, a man shivering in shirtsleeves under the viaduct in Salt Lake City. Ed was there for all of them.

At Ed's funeral, speaker after speaker testified to Ed's gentle, happy, caring service to them. The bishop said that when we moved into the ward, it was as if we had always been there. He said:

> They didn't wait for us to come to them. They came to us. Ed crossed the fence lines and the invisible lines of age, gender, and religion until he had met everyone in the neighborhood. Ed was able to get more mileage out of a tiny bag of fortune cookies than the combined empires of Asia realized with gunpowder.

You need to realize that Ed's signature was fortune cookies. He never went anywhere without a plastic bag or two full of fortune cookies in his pockets. He gave them out to the children in his home-teaching families, to the person who came to read the electrical meter—you name it!

Bishop Gaykowski continued:

> When my own grandchildren would come to visit, they would race up the stairs and say, "Hi, Grandma. Hi, Grandpa. Can we go see Ed and Chieko?" Ed would give them fortune cookies and then take them out to the front yard where he had a goodly supply of snails and would help them catch snails and put them in a jar to bring home.

Kjaristy Griffiths also spoke at Ed's funeral; she was a seventeen-year-old in a family that Ed was assigned to home teach. She said:

> Brother Okazaki . . . didn't talk down to us or refuse to

discuss seriously the principles of the gospel. He was prepared to teach and excited to teach. The very first time he came, he pulled out a small notebook and wrote down all of our names, ages, years in school, even my dog's name.

One of our missionaries also spoke at Ed's funeral. He talked about how nervous and anxious he and the other missionaries in his district in Okinawa were the first time Ed came to interview them. They just barely knew his name and that he was from Hawaii. Would he be harsh and demanding? or fair and kind? Their questions were answered in the first few seconds. Our missionary said:

> The first time I saw our new mission president was from the airport observation deck on the island of Okinawa. We saw a short man with a big smile carrying his own suitcase across the tarmac. He looked up at us, grinned, waved and shouted, "You guys look like a million bucks!"
>
> We discovered that we had an unusual leader. He was completely free of the pompous solemnity sometimes found in the Church.

Then our missionary described some of the ways Ed served the missionaries:

> He let us know we were important. He greeted the groups of new missionaries at the airport by rolling out a piece of red carpet for them to stand on while he shook their hands, with a chorus of local members singing in the background. To missionaries who were struggling with the work, their testimonies, or personal difficulties, he was incredibly patient, respectful, and kind. Those most troubled were sometimes assigned to the mission office where he could try to help them and provide time and space for them to work through their problems. Although our

mission had its full share of problems, *no one* was sent home a failure during the Okazaki years.

When he visited us in our branches he came with a smile and bearing gifts, often a cake or cookies baked by Sister Okazaki. Sometimes he came without warning early in the morning to check on who was up on time and who wasn't. He didn't preach or condemn—he laughed at the ones caught in bed and sometimes stayed to cook breakfast for them.

There were plenty of other ways Ed served, too. During our first winter in Salt Lake City, he was impressed by how promptly our streets were plowed and took up a collection among the neighbors. Then he delivered a box of oranges and a box of apples to the flabbergasted and delighted street crew. He quietly showed up to help feed the homeless. After one of my talks in the ward of one of our missionaries, I looked around for Ed. He was quietly folding up the chairs and tables and putting them away. He made no distinction between important and unimportant service, between important and unimportant people. He gave a four-year-old child or an eighty-year-old widow exactly the same total attention and love that he gave President Kimball or President Hinckley. In fact, it's hard to say, but maybe the four-year-old and the widow got a little bit more. For Ed, the commandment "Inasmuch as ye have done it unto one of the least of these my brethren, you have done it unto me" (Matthew 25:40) was a reflex. He followed the Christian way through his service.

CONCLUSION

Seeing a Mother Teresa or an Ed in action is a way to see Christ in action. I think of Jesus explaining to Philip: "He that hath seen me hath seen the Father." (John 14:9.) When we see a true Christian in action, we see Christ in action. We see Christianity in action when we see any Christian's firsthand relationship with the Savior, a relationship based on continual and loving prayer. Second, we see the way of the Christian in acts of service that are untainted and unencumbered by the burden of judgment.

I will conclude with Ed's own testimony to the young women of Lambda Delta Sigma, because at that point in his remarks, he applied what could have been a tribute to me to all of them. He said:

> To me, Chieko is the most wonderful woman in the world, but I know she is not unique. The Lord has his hand upon each of his children in great lovingkindness. The Lord loves you as much as he loves Chieko. He will make miracles happen for you, as much as for Chieko and me. You will have hard experiences to go through, but he will sustain you in those experiences as he has sustained us. You will make plans and see things sometimes go wrong; but if you take these setbacks with faith, do your very best under all circumstances, and do all the good you can with the skills and abilities you have, I testify that you, too, will be able to look back and see in clarity the Lord's plan for you. I testify that our Heavenly Father does have a plan for each of us, that he loves us, that we must have faith and be obedient to the promptings of the Spirit that come to us directly and also that come to us through the promptings of those who work with us and preside over us.

CHAPTER 8

For Such a Time As This:
Faith in the Savior

The concept of being chosen for a particular time is powerfully illustrated in the book of Esther. (See Esther 4:14.) Her experience seems very real to me. It shows that even a woman who is a queen has to operate within real limitations, that leaders are not always wise or fair, and that malice and hatred can bring misery to many. You remember that the words "for such a time as this" are spoken by Esther's uncle, Mordecai. He and Esther were sending messages back and forth through a harem eunuch because, once Esther had entered the house of women, she could never have direct contact with another man besides the king. Mordecai explained Haman's plot to destroy all the Jews on a certain day so that their property could be confiscated by their murderers. Mordecai begged Esther to plead their cause with the king. From his perspective, she seemed to be a woman with power, with access to the supreme decision-maker, someone the king would have to listen to respectfully.

From her perspective, things seemed much riskier. She was the queen, but she was completely dependent on the king. He had deposed Vashti, his first queen, because she had refused to parade for him and his drunken nobles during a

116

feast that had lasted for many days. Esther had been chosen apparently just for her beauty. She had no powerful family. She represented no important political alliance. She was not even the mother of the king's son and heir. And, as this story shows, the king was very capricious, easily bored, and impulsive. By law, it was death for anyone to enter the king's presence without an invitation. She would be saved only if he extended his scepter to her. Had true love reformed the king? Did Esther have any evidence that he had become any less impulsive, any more responsible and statesmanlike? Not exactly. Furthermore, he had not sent for her for thirty days. Did that mean he was already growing tired of her? After all, he had access to hundreds of other women. Haman was very powerful. He had the king's ear and influenced him easily, even in foolish directions. In fact, Haman already hated Mordecai, because Mordecai refused to pay him royal homage when Haman swept by in his chariot. If the connection between Esther and Mordecai became known, wouldn't Esther be exposed to actual danger of her life?

When she expressed these doubts to Mordecai, he answered in a way that forced her to face her fears:

> Think not with thyself that thou shalt escape in the king's house, more than all the Jews.
> For if thou altogether holdest thy peace at this time, then shall there enlargement and deliverance arise to the Jews from another place; but thou and thy father's house shall be destroyed: and who knoweth whether thou art come to the kingdom for such a time as this? (Esther 4:13–14)

There was a mostly happy ending to the story. The king willingly extended his scepter of acceptance to Esther, listened to her story, and granted her petition. Haman, the enemy of the Jews, was exposed for his treachery and hanged, the Jews took revenge on those who would have slaughtered them, and Mordecai rose to a position of great influence with the king. I can't help wishing that Mordecai and Esther had shown themselves magnanimous and forgiving. Still, it's satisfying to see evil thwarted so decisively.

Recalling the story of Esther in the context of strengthening our testimonies of Jesus Christ, I'd like to focus on two qualities that seemed very important to both Esther and Mordecai and also to us. These qualities are faith and service.

FAITH

First, the story of Esther teaches us about faith. The quality of Esther's faith is realistic. It's not based on sweet sentiments or pretty feelings. She knows exactly what the risks are. She faces squarely the possibility that she may die as a result of her efforts to help her people. This is a life-and-death situation. She knows that God *can* help her, but she doesn't know if God *will* help her in this particular situation. It is in that context of doubt and uncertainty that she exercises her faith.

Sometimes we struggle with God's agency as much as we struggle with our own. How can God refuse to answer our petitions? How can we know what his will is? How can he permit the tears and prayers of frightened children who are being sexually or physically abused to rise up before him and not answer their pleadings for deliverance? These are questions I have often pondered, and I have no easy answers. I do know, however, that if God were not free—if he had no choice about granting or not granting our prayers—then we would not be free either. I believe that there is a terrible accountability for those who abuse their agency by abusing others, but that accountability will be exacted at a later time.

What I'm saying is that faith is not the same as magic. God is not a vending machine. He does not give us candy bars when we feed in a prayer. I love a wonderful little letter to God written by a first- or second-grade girl. This little girl wrote: "Dear God, are you real? Some people do not believe it. If you are you better do something quick. Harriet Ann." (*Children's Letters to God,* comp. Eric Marshall and Stuart Hample, enl. ed. [New York: Pocket Books, 1975], n.p.)

God isn't in the business of making us believe him. Faith cannot exist if there is no freedom to doubt. And freedom means that terrible mistakes will be made. I don't believe that faith means God will remove all tragedies from our path or solve all of our problems for us. I believe it means that he will be with us, suffering with us and grieving with us and working with us as we deal with our own tragedies and work our way through those problems.

Dr. Olga Kovářová joined the Church in Czechoslovakia in 1983, the first young person in that country to be baptized in more than forty years. Since the imposition of Communist rule after World War II, the Church had been outlawed. To be caught in a meeting, even in a private home, to be baptized, to discuss the scriptures, to perform a priesthood ordinance—any one of these offenses could bring with it a prison sentence of three to seven years. She was a professor of philosophy and ethics; but instead of teaching Marxism-Leninism, she taught a system of trust, responsibility, and love based on the Book of Mormon scripture, "Men are that they might have joy." She conducted yoga camps during the summer where she reached hundreds of young people.

Olga lived in Bratislava, the second largest city in Czechoslovakia. Her little branch had only seven members when she first began attending meetings. By 1989, the year of Czechoslovakia's "velvet revolution," there were about sixty members. She talked about their meetings—of slipping into a private home after dark, having all the windows closed, the blinds pulled down, never singing a hymn. Their manuals were forty years old. There was one Book of Mormon, and it rotated to each in turn. When it was Olga's turn to have it, she stayed up all night reading it.

Olga, like all of the members, was interrogated many times by the secret police, the first time when she was twenty-two or twenty-three. She said that she went into that interrogation thinking, "I could be in prison until I am thirty." And she prayed. She prayed very hard for the Lord's protection. She said, "Do you know what it is like, being called into a room where there are six people, sitting at a table, asking you questions?" Think of the fear she had to face, like Esther, and how she must have mustered her faith for that undertaking.

Another example Olga Kovářová used was that of the coin. We think of a coin as having only two sides—heads or tails. She pointed out that the coin has a third side—the edge. She compared one side of the coin to the view that all reality is material and physical, the other to the spiritual reality. And the edge holds both sides together. It is narrow and inconspicuous, easy to overlook, but we live our lives on that edge, drawing from both the material and the spiritual. We know from the scriptures that from the eternal perspective of the Lord, "all things unto [God] are spiritual" (D&C 29:34), but that is a perspective that we as mortals must struggle to achieve perfectly in this life. We live in a physical world and deal with physical realities. We also live in a spiritual world and deal with spiritual realities. Our lives have both sides. We must honor and acknowledge both the material and the spiritual realities in our lives and find ways for them to work together.

The key to keeping these two realities together lies in Christ. We must cling to Christ with all of the energy and power of our heart, might, mind, and strength. There will always be problems in relationships until we start getting our messages from the Savior instead of from people who are just as scared and limited as we. There have been many days in my life when I could speak only with Heavenly Father and tell him what I really felt. My faith came out of those lonely times when I knew that Heavenly Father was with me—not removing difficulties from my path but walking beside me and sharing those difficulties with me.

Zina Diantha Huntington Young, who was Relief Society general president from 1888 to 1901, said: "Seek for a testimony, as you would, my dear sisters, for a diamond concealed. If someone told you by digging long enough in a certain spot you would find a diamond of unmeasured wealth, do you think you would begrudge time or strength or means spent to obtain that treasure? Then I will tell you that if you will dig in the depths of your own hearts you will find with the aid of the Spirit of the Lord, the pearl of great price, the testimony of the truth of this work." ("Voices of Faith," *Ensign*, Mar. 1992, p. 8.)

We do not know how Esther developed her faith in the Lord, but she had that diamond, that treasure. We, too, can develop that same quality of faith, and we will need it for such a time as this. Esther's faith gave her courage. She faced death to save her people. Her courage came from her faith in the Lord, and so does ours. I simply don't know any way to muster the courage we need to handle our problems other than going to the Lord in faith.

I cherish a stitchery given to me by a Relief Society president in Upland, California, with this motto on it: "This day, nothing will come my way that God and I cannot handle." I want to tell you that I have seen days in my life—and I'm certain that you've seen days in your life as well—when God has had to carry more than his share of the burden. But he has always done so.

We all have challenges to face that test our courage. I want you to know that the Savior is with us in our difficult moments. And I urge you to take courage and be of good cheer. It's hard enough to bear our burdens and go about our duty without weighting our steps down even more by a downcast countenance and by a mournful consciousness of how sad we are. I'm not saying we should put on a facade or lie to ourselves or others, but I am saying that we should choose the path of courage and cheer just as much as we possibly can. It will strengthen us. And we certainly don't need to take on the totally unnecessary burden of inappropriate guilt and feelings of inadequacy that come from comparing ourselves to others.

SERVICE

Service is the second aspect of the story of Esther. It's very significant to me that Esther exercised her faith to perform an act of service. Mordecai was probably wrong. She would have been safe in the king's house, especially since her nationality was a secret. But her desire to serve her people was stronger than her desire for safety and comfort. She took the risk because she accepted service as her right and her responsibility.

Sometimes opportunities present themselves as risk, discomfort, and inconvenience. It was a scary thing to accept our calling to the Japan Okinawa Mission in 1968; but God honored our willingness to serve, our courage in taking the risk, and our faith that he would help us do his work, and we were able to serve with joy and freedom in that mission.

Mother Teresa of Calcutta tells about her own philosophy of service. A wealthy Australian visited her some time ago and said that he wanted to give her a big donation. She truly feels that people are happiest when they are sharing, so she accepted the donation graciously, as if she were doing him a favor. Then without a word or a suggestion from her, the next miracle happened. This Australian didn't seem satisfied by giving her the money. He said, "This is something outside of me, but I want to give something of *me.*" He began going regularly to the Home for the Dying, shaving the men who were well enough, and talking to them. Of course, he could have spent that time on himself, just as he could have spent the money on himself. But he wanted to give something of himself. For Mother Teresa, the miracle was very simple. She says:

> I never speak to them of money or ask for things from them. I just ask them to come and love the people, to give their hands to serve them and their hearts to love them. And when they come in touch with them, then their first impulse is to do something for them. And next time they come,

they're already involved. When they have been for some time in Calcutta or in any other place, they feel that they are part of the people. [They realize] . . . how lovable these people are, just [as] they are and how much they can give to them. (Malcolm Muggeridge, *Something Beautiful for God: Mother Teresa of Calcutta* [New York: Walker and Co./ Phoenix Press, 1971; large print ed., 1984], pp. 116–17)

That is quiet service, simple service, unspectacular service. Esther's service was very spectacular. She saved a whole people from genocide. Probably none of us will ever be in a dramatic situation that is even remotely similar. Our opportunities to serve come one at a time, person by person. I hope that in addition to the projects where we work en masse to accomplish great purposes, there are also quiet personal projects where we see the face of the person we are serving and where, in our own eyes, smiling back at them, they can see the love of the Savior.

I think that Esther, through her faith, through her courage, and through her service, found out who she truly was. If it had not been for her generous service, even when it represented a great risk, we would remember her, if we knew about her at all, just as a pretty Jewish girl who won a national beauty contest and got to be queen for life instead of queen for a day. There is something about service that discloses our eternal identity to ourselves, that brings us into harmony with the Savior in a way that lets our eternal identity shine through all of the mortal distractions.

Think again of Mother Teresa and how true that is of her. Malcolm Muggeridge, the prize-winning journalist who has made documentaries about Mother Teresa, talks about how extraordinarily real and vivid she is:

There is much talk today [he says] about discovering an identity, as though it were something to be looked for, like a winning number in a lottery; then, once found, to be hoarded and treasured. . . . With Mother Teresa, in effacing herself, she becomes herself. I never met anyone more memorable. Just meeting her for a fleeting moment makes an ineffaceable impression. I have known people burst into tears when she goes, though it was only from a tea party where their acquaintance with her amounted to no more than receiving her smile.

He tells of driving her and one of her sisters to the Calcutta railway station very early in the morning in his absurdly large American limousine. On the way, they passed the sleeping figures of the hundreds of homeless who filled the street. The porters rushed forward, expecting rich Americans, and then fell back. They recognized the cheap white saris with blue bands that the Sisters of Charity wore. Mother Teresa and her companion carried all of their luggage in a simple handbasket. Muggeridge settled them in their third-class compartment, trying to be sure they were comfortable:

When the train began to move, and I walked away, I felt as though I were leaving behind me all the beauty and all the joy in the universe. Something of God's universal love has rubbed off on Mother Teresa, giving her homely features a noticeable luminosity; a shining quality. She has lived so closely with her Lord that the same enchantment clings about her that sent the crowds chasing after him in Jerusalem and Galilee, and made his mere presence seem a harbinger of healing. Outside, the streets were beginning to stir; sleepers awakening, stretching and yawning; some raking over the piles of garbage in search of something edible. It was a scene of desolation, yet it, too, seemed somehow

125

irradiated. This love, this Christian love, which shines down on the misery we make, and into our dark hearts that make it; irradiating all, uniting all, making of all one stupendous harmony. Momentarily I understood. (*Something Beautiful for God,* pp. 3–5)

The mystery is love. All our faith, all our courage, and all our service come together in an expression of love focused on the Savior. We do not know how Esther understood God or what faith she had in the Messiah to come. But we feel connected to her by her faith, her courage, and her service.

CONCLUSION

Let us build upon our own faith and our own service. We can understand the mystery of Christian love that shines into the darkness around us and into the darkness of hearts and unites us with others. We can feel the steadfast and joyful love of the Savior in our hearts. Like Esther, we can respond with faith to the challenges we face, even if they seem too large and too complicated for us. We can find courage, even when trials beset us and our world seems dark. We can reach outside our small circles and take the risk of serving others. Like Mother Teresa, we can see the needs not only for food and shelter but for human kindness and divine love.

Esther was a queen, but all of us have the potential of being kings and queens, priests and priestesses, gods and goddesses. Like Esther we are called to live with faith and with service. We, too, whatever our circumstances, must meet those circumstances as queens and kings who are called and challenged to be here in this hour.

CHAPTER 9

And Be Perfected in Him

Moroni 10:32 calls to all of us, "Come unto Christ, and be perfected in him." This passage comes from a section of scriptures written to the "daughter of Zion." Let's put ourselves in the place of those to whom this scripture is addressed as we read.

> And again I would exhort you that ye would come unto Christ, and lay hold upon every good gift, . . .
>
> Awake, and arise from the dust, O Jerusalem; yea, and put on thy beautiful garments, O daughter of Zion; and strengthen thy stakes and enlarge thy borders forever, that thou mayest no more be confounded, that the covenants of the Eternal Father which he hath made unto thee, O house of Israel, may be fulfilled.
>
> Yea, come unto Christ, and be perfected in him, and deny yourselves of all ungodliness; and if ye shall deny yourselves of all ungodliness, and love God with all your might, mind and strength, then is his grace sufficient for you, that by his grace ye may be perfect in Christ. (Moroni 10:30–32)

One of the reasons I love this scripture is that it tells me to be perfect "in Christ." I don't think that is the same thing as being perfect in everything. Being perfect in Christ is not the same thing as being perfect in paying my tithing, plus being perfect in attending sacrament meeting every week with panty hose that *never* have runs, plus being perfect in doing all of the housecleaning (including the windows) every week, plus being perfect in closing multi-million-dollar deals for multinational corporations, plus being perfect in having children who never misbehave, plus being perfect in whatever personal items we all carry around on our righteousness checklists. Instead, this scripture talks about being perfected in Christ. To me being perfected in Christ means accepting the atonement of Christ by relying on the Savior's love and abiding in the path of prayer to let that atonement work in me.

RELYING ON THE SAVIOR'S LOVE

The image of the path is a useful one, because it teaches us that there is a way by which we may come to our Savior. But in another way it is misleading. Paths lead from one point to another. The image suggests that we are over here and the Savior is over there and that we must follow the path to reach him. It implies that there is a distance between us and the Lord and that we must traverse that difference to find ourselves with him. Yet, in reality, he is already with us. Yes, there is a path, and yes, we do have far to go; but the Savior is walking beside us on the path already, prepared to go with us the whole distance. Isaiah 42:16 records the Savior's promise to us: "And I will bring the blind by a way that they knew not; I will lead them in paths that they have not known: I will make darkness light before them, and crooked things straight. These things will I do unto them, and not forsake them." He is beside us, even when we cannot see him in our blindness. He

128

is making crooked things straight before us. He is lighting our darkness. And he will not forsake us.

I think President Thomas S. Monson is one of the people who have this sense of the Savior's guidance and presence. When President Monson was interviewed by the *Church News*, he talked about the Savior's desires as the single most important principle in his life. All of the paintings in his office are owned by the Church, except for one portrait representing the Savior:

> "I've had that picture since I was a bishop, when it was on the wall facing me in my office for five years," he said. "I had it at home when I was a stake presidency member. I took it to Canada with me, and had it when I was a mission president. I brought it to this building when I was called as an apostle. I've occupied two or three rooms in this building, but that picture has always been on the wall facing me. There isn't a day that I'm here that I don't come up against difficult decisions, those that require wisdom beyond my own. It's very typical for me to look at that picture and ask, 'What would He do?'
>
> "I find if I put that preamble in my mind I don't have much difficulty in providing counsel, in making decisions, in planning a course of action." (Gerry Avant, "Approaching a Milestone Event," *Church News*, 15 Aug. 1992, p. 6)

I think President Monson's principle or preamble of asking, "What would He do?" is a wonderful and powerful one. What better way to invite the influence of the Savior into our lives than to consciously ask ourselves, "What decision would Jesus make now? How would he greet this person who is approaching me? How would he speak to this child who has just tipped over his milk for the third meal in a row?" It's a principle that's parallel to the Golden Rule, which asks us to ask ourselves, "How would we like to be treated or spoken to right now by this person?" When Mother Teresa of Calcutta is asked how she can continue to serve the poor so selflessly, she tells of her own experiences with hunger, thirst, fatigue, and poverty. She was teaching in a comfortable and pleasant girls' school when finally, after many years of application and effort, she was released from her order and allowed to pursue the ministry among the poor that she felt burning in her heart. She left the school with very little:

> I was on the street, with no shelter, no company, no helper, no money, no employment, no promise, no guarantee, no security.
>
> Then I prayed, "My God, you, only you. I trust in your call, your inspiration. You will not let me down."
>
> I needed a roof to shelter the abandoned, so I started to search.
>
> I walked and walked all the time, until I couldn't walk any more.
>
> Then I understood better the exhaustion of the really poor, always in search of a little food, of medicines, of everything.
>
> The memory of the material security that I enjoyed in the convent of Loreto came then to me as a temptation and I prayed like this:
>
> "O God, through free choice and through your love, I want to stay here and do your will. No, I cannot go back. My community are the poor. Their security is mine. Their health is my health. My home is the home of the poor: not just of the poor, but of those who are the poorest of the poor. Of those to whom one tries not to get too close for fear of catching something, for fear of the dirt, or because they are covered in germs and disease. Of those that do not go to

pray because they can't leave their houses naked. Of those that no longer eat because they haven't the strength. Of those that fall in the streets, knowing that they are going to die, while the living walk by their sides ignoring them. Of those who no longer cry, because they have no tears left. Of the untouchables." (José Luis González-Galado and Janet N. Playfoot, *My Life for the Poor: Mother Teresa of Calcutta* [San Francisco: Harper & Row, 1985], p. 10)

Her compassion for the poor springs from her deep identification with the Savior and with the poor themselves. She relies on the Savior's inexhaustible and unquenchable love to make her own love never-failing.

I can't tell you how immensely comforting this idea is to me. I don't have to rely on my own goodness to be good. I can rely on the Savior's goodness filling my heart when I am worthy and willing to receive it. I don't have to rely on my own capacity for love to be loving. I can rely on the Savior's love to fill my heart so completely that it will brim over and spill irresistibly into love for the people around me. I don't have to rely on my own patience, my own generosity, my own forgiveness, or my own steadfastness to be patient, generous, forgiving, or steadfast in righteousness. If I am willing to make room in my heart for the Savior, if I invite him into my life, and if I fix my thoughts and desires and hopes on him, then in some miraculous way, I can think the thoughts of Jesus, I can feel the feelings of Jesus, and I can do the works of Jesus.

This is not a complicated idea. It is the joyful promise made to all those who are willing to take the name of Jesus upon them and who covenant, with full seriousness of heart, that they want his Spirit to always be with them. Remember what Nephi reminds those who have been baptized and have thus entered what he calls "this strait and narrow path":

> Wherefore, ye must press forward with a steadfastness in Christ, having a perfect brightness of hope, and a love of God and of all men. Wherefore, if ye shall press forward, feasting upon the word of Christ, and endure to the end, behold, thus saith the Father: Ye shall have eternal life. (2 Nephi 31:19–20)

We can rely on Christ to be with us on the path that leads to perfection in Christ. We can live our lives in the "perfect brightness of hope" that Nephi talks about. We can have perfect confidence in His promise to be with us. As Psalm 16:11 says, "Thou wilt shew me the path of life: in thy presence is fulness of joy; at thy right hand there are pleasures for evermore."

FOLLOWING THE PATH OF PRAYER

The second point that I think is important in understanding what it means to be perfect in Christ is to realize that we cannot make very much progress on that path unless we fill our hearts with prayer. Prayer is definitely a duty. We are commanded to have family prayer twice a day, to ask the Lord's blessings on the food that we eat, to open and close meetings with prayer, and to pray as families, in groups, and singly. But prayer is also a delight, an ongoing conversation with our Heavenly Father, an ongoing recognition of the presence of the Holy Ghost, and a continued, joyful awareness of the Savior's love in our lives.

Let me quote two very short letters to God from children.

(*Children's Letters to God*, comp. Eric Marshall and Stuart Hample, enl. ed. [New York: Pocket Books, 1975], n. p.)

The first is from a little girl, perhaps in the second or third grade, named Martha. She writes anxiously: "I'm sorry I did not write before but I only learned how this week." I think that this child's words unconsciously reveal, even at this early age, a "duty" orientation to prayer. It's an obligation, a responsibility, a duty—and already she's apologizing and feeling guilty because she hasn't done it right. Do we ever do that to ourselves? And how do you think Heavenly Father feels when we come to him feeling anxious, apologetic, and afraid? Is that how he wants us to feel?

The second letter is from a little girl named Sue. She writes: "Dear God, Why do I have to pray when you know anyway what I want? But I'll do it if it makes you feel better." Now *that's* the spirit. Here's an honest little girl who is saying, "I have a question. There's something here I don't understand." But she's also saying something about what's really important—and that's her relationship with God. I think when she grows a little older she will realize that God isn't the only one who felt better when she prayed to him and that there are other messages in prayer besides what she wants. Most important, I think that we can predict a long, healthy, and happy relationship with God for Sue because it's based on honesty and love. But I worry about Martha. How healthy is a relationship based on guilt? I won't ask you how long it can last, though, because we all know that guilt-based relationships can last our whole lives!

The point I want to make is that these two approaches affect not only our prayers but all of our lives. Duties are important. They're nearly always opportunities to serve. But they should be delightful to us as well, stars to steer by, not sticks to beat ourselves with. The message of the Atonement is that Jesus suffered and died for us while we were still sinners. He is willing to meet us where we are. Christ's redemptive sacrifice was for all humankind, but it was also for each one of us individually. I think that Christ would still have accomplished the Atonement if only one human being on the face of the earth needed that sacrifice. Each one of us has infinite worth. Prayer should be our first recourse when we find our duties turning into drudgery instead of delights. I'm astonished, sometimes, when I'm sitting with a sister who is telling me the many problems and difficulties she is coping with. I will ask her, "And how do you feel when you pray about this?" Often, the answer is: "I haven't prayed about it." The reason I'm astonished is that I can't imagine how I could *help* praying about it. I pray about my days and my nights, my meetings and my solitudes. I pray for friends in difficulty and for strangers who catch my eye. I pray when I'm pushing a shopping cart, when I'm driving, when I'm in elevators.

Obviously these prayers are prayers of the heart, not formal kneeling prayers. Maybe some would think they're not quality-time prayers. Well, I subscribe to the quantity-time prayer theory as well. They're the path on which I find the Savior waiting for me. Some of the people I've talked to have confessed, "I guess one of the reasons I haven't prayed is that I'm afraid of what I'll hear." I'm *never* afraid of what I'll hear because I know it will come in the tones of love. I'm hungry for more. I also don't think that the Lord overrides our agency by giving us flat commands. He respects our agency, wants us to learn to make decisions, and wants us to share all of our lives with him, not just meet for a summit conference every couple of weeks or so. I think that prayer is both a way to make miracles happen and also a way to recognize the miracles that are already happening in our lives.

Do you feel that you don't have time to pray? Are you snatching a few minutes at bedtime and in the morning and saying the blessing with one hand on the telephone and another one carrying a sandwich to your mouth? I suggest that in addition to regular times of kneeling prayer you find times when

> the body is busy but the mind is not. . . . One man . . . prays as he mows his lawn. Another prays while he is refinishing furniture. And a woman speaks to God while she washes, folds, and irons clothing for her family of seven. A busy mother of three who also works as the public relations director of a large corporation prays during her hour-long commute in the morning. "There are no interruptions at all," she says, "no kids calling for me, and no telephone ringing."

Another suggestion is to pray while waiting in lines, taking literally the invitation from Psalm 37:7 that says "Rest in the Lord, and wait patiently for him." One man found himself in a long, tedious bank line. Rather than be impatient, he began to pray for people he knew who had special needs. He writes:

> No sooner had I started praying than I noticed that a woman seated at one of the desks was quietly weeping.
> Leaving my place in line, I made my way to her. I said that I could see she was upset and wondered if I could help. She told me that day was the first anniversary of her college-aged son's death . . . of leukemia.

I listened as she talked for a few minutes. When she was through, she thanked me repeatedly for allowing her to share her sadness, telling me she felt much better because of our conversation. When I waited on the Lord while waiting in line, He spoke to me—directing me to someone in need. (Victor Parachin, "Real Prayer for Real People," *Signs of the Times,* July 1992, p. 10)

I firmly believe there is no problem we cannot take to the Lord in prayer. Here's an example:

Ann, a mid-level manager at a large consulting firm, had a problem employee who was persistently late, even though punctuality was a cardinal rule of the firm. Ann would talk to Molly, Molly would promise to do better, but nothing would change. It was getting conspicuous. Ann worried that people would think she was favoring Molly. Was she going to have to fire her to get her attention? Then at church [she was not LDS], she joined with the congregation in singing "What a Friend We Have in Jesus," and Ann had this remarkable experience:

When they came to the line [in the hymn], "What a privilege to carry everything to God in prayer," Ann almost gasped aloud. She hadn't thought of praying about this frustrating matter.

After the worship service, Ann went directly to her office, knelt by her desk, prayed about the problem, [and] then . . . went home.

The results were amazing. On Monday morning, [Molly] arrived promptly at 8:00 A.M., and she has continued to be on time since. (Ibid., p. 8)

I was very interested to read a report from a Harvard cardiologist who had found in his work that

people who feel themselves in touch with God are less likely to get sick—and better able to cope when they do. . . . Simple prayers produce what he calls the "relaxation response," bringing benefits by reducing hypertension, headaches, and other pain. . . . Prayer doesn't just work for the person who's praying. It also works when a person is praying for someone else. A feature article in *Newsweek* about prayer . . . told about an experiment a researcher conducted at San Francisco General Hospital. . . . The researcher asked outsiders to pray for a group of cardiac patients. The study found that even though the patients weren't told someone was praying for them, "they recovered faster than those in an otherwise identical control group." (David C. Jarnes, "The Prescription Is Prayer," *Signs of the Times*, July 1992, p. 8)

Now that's an interesting report, isn't it? I suppose you could call it scientific evidence, if we needed such evidence, of the efficacy of prayer.

And here's another miracle, a miracle not only of prayer but also of love. Polly Adams of Show Low Third Ward in Arizona, writing in the *Church News*, told about her father, Carl L. Vance, who had spent eight years working on his family history and had found everything he needed except his parents' marriage certificate. He had looked everywhere, canvassed relatives and friends, even driven to their county courthouse in South Dakota to try and find it. Without it, he could not have them sealed. Then in July 1991, he was at the county dump to unload a pickup full of yard cuttings. When he kicked a board out of his way, he saw underneath it an old, oil-smeared envelope. Curious, he picked it up, and saw that the return address said "Pierre, South Dakota." The envelope bore no address, but it had been postmarked 1987. Quickly he opened the partially ripped envelope and, inside, saw his parents' marriage certificate. Polly wrote, "What my father had prayed, hoped for, and [worked] for was right there in his hands at the county landfill." (Polly Adams, "Junkyard Treasure," *Church News*, 6 June 1992, p. 16.)

What a thrill! And what gratitude must have filled his heart. We share such experiences in our families, in our fast and testimony meetings, and in our circles of sisterhood, not because we are amazed at the miracles—though they are amazing—and not to keep people working away at their genealogy—although how could it help but have that effect?—but because they are testimonies of love to us of a Heavenly Father who knows and cares about the concerns of our heart.

I want to read to you a third letter from this collection of children's letters to God. One little girl wrote, "Dear God, Do plastic flowers make you mad? I would be if *I* made the real ones. Lucy." (*Children's Letters to God*, n. p.)

I tend to prefer real flowers to plastic flowers, myself, but I don't think there's necessarily anything evil about plastic flowers unless they're passing themselves off as real flowers. The danger is that unless we have a firsthand relationship with real flowers, we won't be able to tell the difference.

Jesus wants us to have a firsthand relationship with him. Doctrine and Covenants 93, verse 1, promises: "Verily, thus saith the Lord: It shall come to pass that every soul who forsaketh his sins and cometh unto me, and calleth on my name, and obeyeth my voice, and keepeth my commandments, shall see my face and know that I am." He doesn't want us just to be able to quote scriptures about him, to sit in Sunday School classes and listen to lessons about him, or to listen to other people's experiences with him. He wants each one of us, you and me, to forsake our sins, to come to him, to keep his commandments, and to call on his name. And the corresponding promise is also to "every soul"—not just to Joseph Smith or the regional representative or the stake president or the Relief Society president. It's to you, to me. He promises that each one of us "shall see my face and know that I am."

Let's deal with the real flowers, the real voice, the real Spirit. Jesus didn't make mistakes, I think, because he was so fully in tune with his Father. He heard the voice of his Father and thought the thoughts of his Father. When the woman taken in adultery was brought before Jesus, he told her accusers to cast the first stone if they were without sin. How could Jesus have been so wise? Then, as the accusers melted away, he told the woman gently, "Neither do I condemn thee: go, and sin no more." (See John 8:1–11.) A statement that focused on legal correctness but overlooked the eternal principles of repentance would have sounded a sour note compared to the voice of his Father that Jesus heard.

Here's another way to help us understand this same idea. *Se-i,* the Japanese word meaning "holy" or "saintly," is written with three characters derived from the Chinese pictographs, one the word for *ear,* one the word for *mouth,* and one the word for *king.* So a holy person is someone who has her ear near the mouth of the king, so she can hear his voice easily and clearly. Isn't that a lovely way to think about holiness? (See Len Walsh, *Read Japanese Today* [Rutland, Vermont, and Tokyo: Charles E. Tuttle, 1969], p. 131.)

Let's just summarize the five main points I've made about prayer. First, the message of Martha's apologetic letter is that prayer is a duty and a commandment, but, second, the message of Sue's puzzled but willing letter reminds us that prayer is commanded for *our* benefit, not God's. It is a duty but a delightful duty. We should lighten up if we're taking our responsibilities so seriously that they burden and oppress us rather than lift and enlighten us. Third, prayer is an avenue to miracles. Ann, Molly's manager, learned that there is nothing we cannot take to the Lord in prayer. Fourth, prayer for others and the exercise of faith on behalf of others is one of the greatest motivations I can think of to inspire us to lead purer lives. And fifth, one most important reason the Lord has commanded us to pray is so that we can have an authentic, firsthand relationship with him—not a secondhand or artificial relationship.

CONCLUSION

We can rely on Christ. We can trust him and trust his love for us. We can testify with the Nephites of old: "And now, behold, my beloved brethren [and sisters], this is the way; and there is none other way nor name given under heaven whereby [we] can be saved in the kingdom of God." (2 Nephi 31:21.)

Let us take seriously the Savior's confidence and trust in us, too. Speaking to the early Saints in this dispensation, he said: "Therefore, gird up thy loins for the work. Let thy feet be shod also, for thou art chosen, and thy path lieth among the mountains, and among many nations." (D&C 112:7.)

May we walk the path that is the Savior's way and recognize his companionship along that way. May we accept the Savior and his infinite and eternal sacrifice on our behalf. May we invoke his power in our lives and, with all simplicity of heart, accept the reality of his love for us. May we develop that relationship through prayer until our sense of Christ's presence in our lives is a real power, and may we feel that strength upholding us as we deal with our moments of adversity.

CHAPTER 10

Steadfast in Christ

As I pondered various scriptures that deal with the topic of being steadfast, I was particularly struck by the lovely promise that the Lord gave to the Saints of Joseph Smith's day in Doctrine and Covenants 84:60–63:

> Verily, verily, I say unto you who now hear my words, which are my voice, blessed are ye inasmuch as you receive these things;
> For I will forgive you of your sins with this commandment—that you remain steadfast in your minds in solemnity and the spirit of prayer, in bearing testimony to all the world of those things which are communicated unto you. . . .
> And as I said unto mine apostles, even so I say unto you, . . . ye are they whom my Father hath given me; ye are my friends.

Isn't that glorious! The Savior promises us forgiveness of our sins and calls us his friends if we remain steadfast in prayer and testimony. I'd like to explore how we can be steadfast in prayer and steadfast in service.

STEADFAST IN PRAYER

First, let's discuss what it means to be steadfast in prayer. In the Book of Mormon, Amulek gives some beautiful instructions about how widespread, far-reaching, and all-encompassing our prayers should be:

> Yea, humble yourselves, and continue in prayer unto him.
>
> Cry unto him when ye are in your fields, yea, over all your flocks.
>
> Cry unto him in your houses, yea, over all your household, both morning, mid-day, and evening.
>
> Yea, cry unto him against the power of your enemies. Yea, cry unto him against the devil, who is an enemy to all righteousness.
>
> Cry unto him over the crops of your fields, that ye may prosper in them.
>
> Cry over the flocks of your fields, that they may increase.
>
> But this is not all; ye must pour out your souls in your closets, and your secret places, and in your wilderness.
>
> Yea, and when you do not cry unto the Lord, let your hearts be full, drawn out in prayer unto him continually for your welfare, and also for the welfare of those who are around you. (Alma 34:19–27)

Is there one thing that we could or should exclude from our prayers? Is there any topic about which the Lord doesn't want us to pray? Obviously not. And he makes a distinction between crying unto the Lord—by which I think he means formal prayers, even prayers spoken aloud—and prayers of the heart. I have always loved the image of a full heart, drawn out in prayer to God; and I have learned so much about a heart full of prayer. I have needed the companionship of the Savior so much since my husband's death, so it has been easy for me to have my heart drawn out in prayer—prayers of deep need for that sacred companionship and then prayers of loving gratitude when that companionship comes.

Elder Boyd K. Packer talked about the importance of attuning ourselves to listen to the "quiet voice of inspiration" in our prayers; to illustrate, he described how one of his sons had always been interested in ham radio. Elder Packer cheerfully admits that, as he has sat with this enthusiastic son, speaking to someone in a distant part of the world, he has been amazed and impressed by his son's ability to communicate: "I could hear static and interference and catch a word or two, or sometimes several voices at once. Yet he can understand, for he has trained himself to tune out the interference." ("Prayers and Answers," *Ensign,* Nov. 1979, p. 19.)

He marveled at his son's ability and soon realized that he had a similar one:

> In the early days of our marriage, our children came at close intervals. As parents of little children will know [and I'm sure this is something we can all relate to!], in those years it is quite a novelty for them to get an uninterrupted night of sleep.
>
> If you have a new baby, and another youngster cutting teeth, or one with a fever, you can be up and down a hundred times a night. (That, of course, is an exaggeration. It's probably only twenty or thirty times.)
>
> We finally divided our children into "his" and "hers" for night tending. She would get up for the new baby, and I would tend the one cutting teeth.
>
> One day we came to realize that each would hear only the one to which we were assigned, and would sleep very soundly through the cries of the other.
>
> We have commented on this over the years, convinced that you can train yourself to hear what you want to hear, to see and feel what you desire. (Ibid., p. 20)

We've all had this experience, haven't we? We've scanned

the crowd pouring down the concourse at the airport, and our eye has instantly picked out the figure of our husband from the hundreds we're scanning. Or we can hear our own fourth-grader singing in his school chorus. We can hear the voice of the Spirit in the same way, after we have poured out our hearts in prayer, speaking to us in impressions, in promptings, in gentle whispers, in inclinations in one direction and a turning away from another.

I remember reading several years 'ago the experience of Jerry Lee Turley, who moved with her family to the Hopi Indian reservation in Arizona. It felt very much like a foreign country to her, and she was "stunned" when the branch president called her to be the Primary president. She had never worked in Primary before, her branch had no functioning Primary, and she had no experience working with the Hopi. But Nephi's promise, that "the Lord giveth no commandments . . . save he shall prepare a way" (1 Nephi 3:7), strengthened her, and she accepted the calling. The branch president gave her a list of fifteen women and asked her to choose her counselors by the next Sunday.

She pored over the list again and again that week, praying earnestly for inspiration. But she was struggling even to pronounce the names; and as Sunday drew near, she "had a feeling of panic." It was fast Sunday, and she prayed with real intensity as she fasted that the two women the Lord wanted for counselors would be present the next day and she would know who they were. This is what happened:

> When fast and testimony meeting started . . . very few members were in attendance, but as the meeting progressed, the congregation increased. . . . Early in the meeting a sister came in and sat in front of me, and I was impressed that she

was to be one of my counselors. But what of the other? Each time the door opened I looked, wondering if it would be the other counselor. Finally a lovely sister came in, and I knew she was the one. ("I Saw My Counselors Walk In," *Ensign,* Jan. 1976, p. 55)

You can imagine Sister Turley's relief and her gratitude that the Lord would answer her prayers so directly and unmistakably. When we have sweet experiences of this nature, it strengthens our faith in the Savior until we can pray with joy and rejoicing like the words of the psalmist:

> O God, thou art my God; early will I seek thee: my soul thirsteth for thee, my flesh longeth for thee in a dry and thirsty land, where no water is; . . .
>
> Because thy lovingkindness is better than life, my lips shall praise thee.
>
> Thus will I bless thee while I live: I will lift up my hands in thy name.
>
> My soul shall be satisfied . . . ; and my mouth shall praise thee with joyful lips: . . .
>
> Because thou hast been my help, therefore in the shadow of thy wings will I rejoice. (Psalm 63:1–7)

If we have feelings of joy and love and faith in the Savior, we can cry to the Lord about everything in our lives, like Amulek. We can listen for the Lord's voice, like Elder Packer, and expect answers to our prayers, like Sister Turley. We need to be steadfast in prayer.

STEADFAST IN SERVICE

The second way in which we can be steadfast in Christ is to be steadfast in service. Our service doesn't need to be very elaborate or very complicated. Little, tiny things make a big difference. I remember a Russian proverb: "If everyone gives one thread, the poor man will have a shirt."

One important thing to remember about service is that no matter how little you have, there is still enough to share. Our sisters in the Caracas Venezuela Stake learned that a senior citizens' home had a great need for clothing and food. With compassionate hearts, the sisters collected clothes, made cookies and Christmas cakes, and mixed up hot chocolate. Then one Sunday afternoon, with hearts "filled with enthusiasm and charity," they went to the home for the first time.

They introduced themselves to the attendants and asked to spend a few minutes visiting with the elderly women. When they were shown into the large dormitory room where the women who had no families were assigned, they received "a terrible shock." These women had no clothing at all. "They covered themselves with whatever rags they could find and were curled up like little balls," the sisters wrote. "Several sisters had to leave the room to cry outside. Then they steeled themselves and came back in, and we all dressed the women with stockings, underwear, and whatever clothing we had." The women were desperately grateful not only for the clothing and the cookies and hot chocolate but for the attention and care. They begged the sisters not to leave.

Our correspondent wrote, "We have cried many times over this scene . . . and vowed that we would do everything we could to mitigate the anguish, the loneliness, and the hunger of these little ladies who are our sisters." (Untitled and undated typescript, translated for the Relief Society General Board, 1992. Photocopy in my possession.)

I recently learned about a whole ward of sisters who are

steadfast in performing a quiet, consistent, long-term act of Christian service. Ruth McClure of Orem, Utah, remembers hearing with very mixed feelings the announcement about the change to the consolidated meeting schedule. She was happy that the burden of time and expense would be reduced for members of the Church in scattered wards and stakes, but she realized that she herself had a serious problem. Her daughter has multiple handicaps and is very sensitive to noise and movement. When she is overstimulated, she begins to cry in distress. As a result, this daughter had to be cared for at home while the family was in church. That hadn't been a problem up to this point, because someone was always home during the time that Sister McClure needed to attend Relief Society, but now she was stranded. Her husband was serving in a bishopric of a Brigham Young University ward, her younger son was on his mission, and her two older children were married and living at some distance. There was no one to care for her daughter. Then Marilyn Mansfield, a sister in the Relief Society, asked her, "What will you do?"

Sister McClure answered, "I don't know."

Sister Mansfield said quietly, "Let's see what we can do."

She proposed to the ward Relief Society that each sister take one Sunday a year to watch Sister McClure's daughter. "That way you'll only miss one Sunday," she explained, "and Sister McClure won't have to miss any." They passed around a sign-up sheet and filled it in for the first three months. Sister McClure writes:

> That was over twelve years ago, and the sheet is still being filled every three months by those sweet compassionate sisters. In that time, I have served in a number of callings—once even as Primary president! Our ward has been

divided four times. Each time, the new presidency picks up the challenge. Many have come and gone but the generosity of their spirit lingers in my home. And now I have a much clearer understanding of the Savior's charge to "bear one another's burdens." ("Twelve Years and Counting . . . "; typescript in my possession)

It's like a circle. If we're steadfast in prayer, then we have the connection with Christ that lets his love flow into us and through us so that we can reach out in charity to serve others. Our understanding moves in a spiral. At any point where we begin to understand a gospel principle and live it, we can move forward from that point and learn something new. Even when we come back to a principle we think we understand, we find that we will relate to it in a new way because we are no longer the same person we were. For instance, we can serve people because we love them or we can learn to love them by serving them. This love then comes back into our own life, and we have the Savior's own reward for helping others. As a result, our own faith and trust in the Savior deepens constantly and steadily.

CONCLUSION

These two principles of the gospel are not, of course, the only ways we can be steadfast in Christ; but I think they are foundations upon which we can all build. We are being steadfast in Christ when we are steadfast in prayer and steadfast in service. I love the blessing that King Benjamin gave his people in the Book of Mormon—a blessing that again encourages us to be steadfast:

Therefore, I would that ye should be steadfast and

immovable, always abounding in good works, that Christ, the Lord God Omnipotent, may seal you his, that you may be brought to heaven, that ye may have everlasting salvation and eternal life, through the wisdom, and power, and justice, and mercy of him who created all things, in heaven and in earth, who is God above all. (Mosiah 5:15)

PART 4

Courage for Challenging Times

CHAPTER 11

Rain and Rainbows

There's something wonderful about talking about the goodness and mercy of the Lord toward us. I believe that we can find joy and happiness in spite of our trials. Think of the story of Noah and his family. I find it interesting how the Bible describes conditions on the earth at that time:

> And God looked upon the earth, and, behold, it was corrupt; for all flesh had corrupted his way upon the earth.
>
> And God said unto Noah, The end of all flesh is come before me; for the earth is filled with violence through them. (Genesis 6:12–13)

So the Lord commanded Noah to make an ark, giving him the exact specifications, materials, and how many of each kind of animal, bird, and "creeping thing" to take with him on the ark. Then the Lord repeated both the curse and the promise:

> And, behold, I, even I, do bring a flood of waters upon the earth, to destroy all flesh, wherein is the breath of life, from under heaven; and every thing that is in the earth shall die.
>
> But with thee will I establish my covenant; and thou shalt come into the ark, thou, and thy sons, and thy wife, and thy sons' wives with thee. (Genesis 6:17–18)

I want to stress three aspects of the story of Noah. First, adversity. Rain will fall upon all of us, but we can be preserved by listening to the voice of the Lord and following his counsel. At the same time, that will require endurance and patience. You can't tell me there weren't some difficult moments dealing with a seasick hippopotamus! Second, I want to talk about finding rainbows in our lives by concentrating on the moment, rather than dwelling on the past or worrying about the future. And third, I want to share some thoughts on covenants—not only the covenant of continuity of which the rainbow is a sign but the covenants that are rainbows in our own lives.

ADVERSITY

First, let's consider the rain in our lives. Think about the adversity that Noah and his family faced. The mockery of neighbors. The labor of building the ark. The incredibly complex task of gathering the animals and enough food for them. And then the long seasons of patience that were required of them after the rains began.

Adversity is frequently a call to do something great with our lives. Will Smith, the star of a television show, said that when he was fifteen and his brother twelve, their father assigned them to fix a crumbling fifteen-by-fourteen-foot wall near his business. They had to tear it down, dig a six-foot trench, and rebuild the wall. He thought, "This is impossible. This is totally impossible." He was sure he'd be building that wall for the rest of his life, not just the summer. In fact, it took more than six months to finish it. Years later, his father "explained that when a kid's growing up, he needs to see something that's impossible to do, and then go and do it. . . . There are always going to be walls in life. He helped us get over one, so we'd never be scared to take the first step and try to do the impossible. . . . And, of course, he also got a really nice wall." (In Gail Buchalter, "Then I Heard My Father's Voice," *Parade Magazine,* 2 Feb. 1992, p. 14.)

It's nice to know that we can do something impossible if that's what the situation calls for. And when we stand back and look at the challenge to do the impossible, then it says something to us within when we realize that we also got "a really nice wall" out of the situation.

I remember reading a paragraph once from someone named Ralph Sockman. I don't know who he was or where he said this, but it rings true to me: "There are parts of a ship which, taken by themselves, would sink. The engine would sink. The propeller would sink. [The steel plates that make up the sides would sink.] But when these parts are built together, they float. So with the events of my life. Some have been tragic. Some have been happy. But when they are built together, they form a craft that floats and is going someplace. And I am comforted." Now that's a statement that's relevant to our lives, whether our craft is an ark or a battleship.

I've mentioned the patience that was required of Noah and his family. We talk about "forty days and forty nights" as though they had to live in the ark with all those animals for a month and a half. Well, forty days and forty nights was only a fraction of their endurance. For instance, do you remember that after they went into the ark and closed the door, they were inside the ark for seven days *before* the Flood began? (Genesis 7:10.) Now, would that be a test of faith or what?

Would you decide, about the fifth day, that it would be awfully nice to spend the weekend picking buttercups in the meadow rather than cleaning the elephants' stalls and that maybe Noah had made a big mistake?

Then the rains began. The scripture tells us that on the same day "all the fountains of the great deep [were] broken up, and the windows of heaven were opened." (Genesis 7:11–12.) It was not until the fortieth day of this torrential downpour and flooding that the water was deep enough to "lift [the ark] up above the earth." (Genesis 7:17.) And then "the waters prevailed upon the earth an hundred and fifty days." (Genesis 7:24.) We're up to 197 days so far.

The scripture doesn't tell us how many days it took for the waters to recede, but it says that the ark came to rest on the mountains of Ararat on the seventeenth day of the seventh month (Genesis 8:4), and it took until the first day of the tenth month for the tops of the mountains to become visible. If we hypothesize a month of thirty days—and I realize that there are Bible scholars who make careers out of figuring out the calendar—then we need to add another seventy-three days. Then they waited forty days to send out the raven and the dove, seven more days for the second flight of the dove, who returned with the olive branch, and a final seven days for the third flight. It sounds as if it then took another month plus twenty-seven days before they received the command of the Lord to go forth from the ark. (Genesis 8:3–6, 10, 12–14.) According to my addition, this comes to a total of 401 days. That's a long time to be cooped up in a floating zoo—a year, a month, and six days!

So the story of Noah teaches us that there will be adversity, that it will last a long time, and that it will require reserves of patience that seem superhuman. I'm not telling you that you won't have adversity, any more than I'm telling you that it will be easy to handle. I am telling you that you *can* handle it. But how? That brings me to my next point: living in the present moment.

THE PRESENT MOMENT

We don't hear very much about Noah's wife, but it seems to me that there might have been times when she lay awake at night worrying and wondering—worrying if Noah had understood the revelation correctly, wondering if their sons would be resolute and steadfast, worrying about the families of her daughters-in-law who rejected the message of the ark and therefore condemned themselves to death by the great flood. She probably wondered about her grandchildren and whether there would be enough food to see them through. I think you could say that there was a great deal of stress on the ark and that Noah's wife experienced her share and a little more.

Aren't there times when we're all in similar circumstances? Aren't there times for all of us when we're cooperating with decisions that others have made, trying to make homes under temporary and very trying circumstances, and trying to foresee the future on the basis of very inadequate information? That's a real recipe for stress. How can we handle that kind of adversity? That brings us to the next point I want to make.

Rainbows are magically beautiful in their perfect shape and the soft brilliance of their color, but they are also very temporary. They're a happy accident of light in the right quarter, shining through water droplets that happen to be suspended in the air in just the right place. Obviously they can't last long. So if you ever want to enjoy a rainbow permanently, you'd better buy one of those plastic magnets that you can stick on your refrigerator. The real rainbow is a message to you to stop what you're doing and just look for the few minutes that it will be before you.

That's the suggestion I have for dealing with adversity. Don't deny the rain through a false Pollyanna attitude, or you won't have a rainbow. And don't turn your back on the light, or you won't see the rainbow either. It takes both light and rain to make a rainbow, and it will be there for only a moment. Even in moments of deep adversity and pain, look for your rainbow. It's there somewhere.

Here's a little quiz. (You know I used to be a teacher.) Take the word *stressed*, as in "stressed out." Spell it backwards. What does it spell? That's right. It spells *desserts.* Now isn't there a message for us somewhere in that little fact?

Of course you're going to have dark moments. When they come, I hope you remember to lighten up. If there's a lot of rain in your life, look for the light, too—it's there somewhere—and see a rainbow. There have been many dark moments of grief and loneliness for me since Ed's death, and I know there will be more. But there have been rainbow moments, too—of love and support from colleagues and friends, of a renewed sense of preciousness of family between our sons and me. Rainbow moments of remembering good times with Ed.

Find the rainbow moments in your own life. Did you hear

about the workaholic who was thrown into jail? charged with *resisting a rest*. Take care of yourselves. your job, but that's also your joy in this present moment that is given to you.

What can you do with the present moment? I suggest that you use it to do whatever good you can right where you are. When I was in Japan on a Relief Society assignment, some of the leaders told me a story about President Spencer W. Kimball that I just loved. When he was on one of his last visits there and was quite elderly, he had an exhausting sequence of meetings, yet he had time and patience for everyone. Between meetings, he finally had a chance to slip into the rest room. As the leaders waited for him to come out, they began to worry. It seemed that he had been in there for a long time. They wondered if they should check on him. After all, he was not as strong as he used to be. What if he had slipped and fallen? What if he was having trouble of some kind? What if he had been taken ill suddenly? And when the priesthood brethren went in to see what the difficulty was, do you know what they found? President Kimball, the president of the Church and the Lord's prophet on earth, was painstakingly picking up the used paper towels that had spilled over from a receptacle that was too full. What a great lesson that was for those leaders to seize every opportunity that presented itself to do good.

I read about another couple who looked at their limited circumstances and looked at the great needs in the world around them and chose to make a difference right where they were. Mavis Faucher has lived in the same neighborhood since she and and her husband, Lester, were married fifty-two years ago. Mavis, aged seventy-nine, declared war on the trash on Tulip Street where they live because she just couldn't stand the way the street looked. By the time Lester had been enlisted and they'd cleaned up a block,

> the feeling of seeing a clean street was exhilarating and they knew they could make a difference. Thirty trash bags later, Mavis and Lester had covered six blocks. . . . Just think what the streets could look like if there were more people like the Fauchers who took it upon themselves to roll up their sleeves and make a difference. (Christeen Denning, "People Who Made a Difference: Turning Back Trash and Disorder," *Church News,* 30 Nov. 1991, p. 2)

Sometimes we don't enjoy our church meetings and our associations because we're living in the past—trying to figure out why something worked out differently from what we had thought—or living in the future—worrying about something yet to come. At homemaking meeting, what do you do if you have only eight sisters attend? I think you should concentrate on making those eight so happy that they came and so immersed in sisterhood that they'll want to come back the next month. The time to deal with the problem of the twenty who aren't there is later, not at the expense of the eight who are there.

Sometimes things that seem too overwhelming when you think of undertaking them forever become manageable if you focus on the present: "Just for today, go for a brisk walk. Just for today, make time to be alone. Just for today, wear your seat belt. Just for today, exercise your sense of humor." Maybe you can't promise about tomorrow. Maybe you can't change what happened yesterday. But you do have some control over today. (*Hope Healthletter* 12 [January 1992]: 1.)

Another important principle to help us live in the moment is to concentrate on being, rather than doing. A psychologist told of meeting a woman as she sunbathed on a beautiful beach in Hawaii. The woman knew that he was studying people who seemed to have a hard time experiencing joy and said:

> "My husband is a perfect case study for you."
>
> "Where is he?" the psychiatrist asked.
>
> "Oh, up there somewhere," she answered, pointing to the bright blue sky. . . .
>
> "Oh, I'm sorry," the psychiatrist said, preparing himself for yet another story about health problems, stress, or the failures of modern medicine.
>
> *"You're* sorry?" she answered. "You ought to be married to him. Then you would have something to be sorry about."
>
> "I don't understand," answered the psychiatrist, feeling quite confused and wondering if this woman had been in the sun too long.
>
> "Oh, I see." She explained, "No, he's not dead. He's still busy killing himself. I mean he's up there somewhere hang gliding. Yesterday he went parasailing and jet skiing. The day before he golfed until he had blisters and then he snorkeled for so long that he got a sunburn on the part of his back that was out of the water. He looked just like a red humpbacked whale." . . .
>
> "Well, it sounds like he really enjoys these vacations," the psychiatrist said weakly.
>
> "No way," she replied angrily. . . . "He never enjoys anything, he just keeps doing things. . . ."

Our discussion was suddenly interrupted by a shower of sand. The husband had joined us, sweating and panting. . . .

"Hey, that was great," he said. "I haven't wasted one minute of this trip. I've done every single thing this resort offers. . . . Pam, you miss out on everything. You don't know how to have fun. All you do is sit, rest, walk, and read. Get with it, kid, or you'll never enjoy anything."

The husband noticed a volleyball game in progress . . . and as he ran away yelled back, "See you later. Join me when you're ready to have fun." The psychiatrist could see the sunburn on his back. He was too rushed to feel it then, but he would be in for some real pain later.

Then the psychiatrist explained:

When I work with terminally ill patients I notice that, contrary to popular myth, many of these people choose to sit, to think, to fish, and to stroll during the last months of their lives. They do not typically choose to crowd as much into their remaining days as possible by engaging in constant hectic activity. They create more time by taking time, embracing moments, experiencing being alive rather than urgently trying to live.

To illustrate my point, I ask my patients to try the SDASU technique. This stands for "Sit Down and Shut Up." Just sit quietly for a few minutes without talking, waiting for someone or something, or meditating. Just sit down and be quiet. You will notice immediately that you control time when you stop, sit, and get settled. (Paul Pearsall, *Super Joy: In Love with Living* [New York: Doubleday, 1988], pp. 41–42, 54–55)

I think you *know* what works for you. You already know what will keep you centered in the present moment so that you can endure the elephants with patience, so that you can catch sight of the rainbow even while the rain is still falling. Listen to that voice and follow it.

COVENANTS

It's significant that the story of the Flood could end at any of several points. One might be Noah's successful completion of the ark. After years of labor to construct it, after the mockery of the neighbors and the scorn of former friends, after the tension and ingenuity and even danger of collecting and housing the animals and collecting the food they would need, then comes the climactic moment when the rain begins to fall and the water begins to rise and the ark, shut off from the drowning world outside it, lifts gently from the earth, rocks a little in the water, and begins to float. But that's not where the story ends.

Another point where it might end comes when the forty days and nights of the drumming, dripping rain finally stops and the long days of waiting for the water to recede begins, when the dove and the raven are sent out on their mission of searching for dry land anywhere on that vast liquid horizon where the only solid speck is the ark. Then at last the flood waters recede, and the ark gently comes to rest. Think of the impatience and the frustration as they wait for the water to trickle away into ponds and lakes that dry up into meadows and valleys. And then at last the door is open. That's another place where the story could end. But it doesn't.

The animal passengers of the ark rush away with their own cries of thanksgiving while Noah's family gathers around the altar for their ceremony of thanksgiving and the beginning of a new life upon this freshly baptized earth. But even here the story doesn't end. It doesn't end until the Lord gives the promise of which the rainbow is a token—that he will never again curse the earth with a flood. "I do set my bow in the cloud," the Lord said, "and it shall be for a token of a covenant between me and the earth." That covenant was one of continuity, of binding, of continued relationship. The Lord said:

"While the earth remaineth, seedtime and harvest, and cold and heat, and summer and winter, and day and night shall not cease." (Genesis 9:13; 8:22.)

What covenants have we made? What tokens do we have of the covenants between us and the Lord? One of the lessons my own adversity has taught me is a deeper understanding of my covenants. I had always understood that baptism was the entrance into the Church. I wanted to enter into the Church, and I wanted the gift of the Holy Ghost. But no miraculous occurrences attended my baptism and my confirmation. It was not until I began relying on the Holy Ghost and seeking inspiration day by day and sometimes hour by hour that I became aware in quiet, subtle, wonderful ways of the presence of that comforter. And although I always took great comfort from the promise that the Holy Ghost could be my constant companion, it was not until I was suddenly bereft of Ed, my companion for more than forty years, that I turned with terrible need to that promise of companionship that we are given in the sacrament prayer. I found that companionship there, where I needed it.

Covenants are deceptively simple, clear symbols that we can all grasp intellectually with ease. But only as we live with them and return to them often for meaning in the joyous and sorrowful passages of our lives do we begin to understand how deep their roots go. It's the same way with the temple ordinances. Ed used to speak frequently about the joy of sacrifice, the privilege of consecration. I believe he understood dimensions to those covenants that I have yet to explore. But I think that meaning is there for all of us.

The many levels on which we can understand our

covenants suggests two things to me. First, we cannot judge other people. We do not know where they are in their spiritual journey. There may be parts of the gospel that are a great joy and strength to us but that seem mysterious and uncertain to someone else who is involved in learning about other aspects of the gospel. And second, all experience is for our good because we learn in no other way. I always thought that the Lord was trying to comfort Joseph Smith in his afflictions in Liberty Jail when he gave the Prophet a long catalogue of truly terrible things that could yet happen to him, winding up with this list:

> And if thou shouldst be cast into the pit, or into the hands of murderers, and the sentence of death passed upon thee; if thou be cast into the deep; if the billowing surge conspire against thee; if fierce winds become thine enemy; if the heavens gather blackness, and all the elements combine to hedge up the way; and above all, if the very jaws of hell shall gape open the mouth wide after thee, know thou, my son, that all these things shall give thee experience, and shall be for thy good. (D&C 122:7)

Perhaps you, like me, have read that verse and thought, Is this supposed to be *consoling?* Are we supposed to feel *better* after all this? I now believe that the Savior was not trying to comfort Joseph Smith—at least, not as we would comfort a child by saying, "There, there. Everything will be all right." We are beings who have an eternal and everlasting hunger for truth, and what the Savior was giving Joseph Smith was not a pretty pacifier but the nourishing though hard-to-chew bread of truth.

Experience *is* for our good. Good experience, bad experience, happy experience, painful experience—it's all for our good, and we can accept it, deal with it, come to terms with it, and learn from it because it is part of why we came here. No experience is so painful that the Savior has not been there before us. We cannot have an experience that will destroy us unless we choose to let it. The Savior told Joseph Smith: "Hold on thy way. . . . Thy days are known, and thy years shall not be numbered less; therefore, fear not what man can do, for God shall be with you forever and ever." (D&C 122:9.) That's the Lord's promise to us as well as to Joseph Smith. That is the covenant we make and remake at the sacrament table each Sunday—that we will always remember him and that he will always grant us his Spirit to be with us.

Did you thrill, as I did, to President Howard W. Hunter's message at October 1992 conference? He acknowledged that there are many attitudes and experiences in the world today that will try us and frighten us. In the midst of adversity, of tribulation, and of terror, we have a sure beacon in Christ's love and in the sureness of his triumph over despair and danger. President Hunter told the story of the apostles, setting out at night across the Sea of Galilee while Jesus remained in a secluded spot on the shore for prayer and communion with his Father:

> The night was dark and the elements were strong and contrary. The waves were boisterous and the wind was bold, and these mortal, frail men were frightened. . . .
>
> [But] as always [Jesus], was watching over them. He loved them and cared for them. In their moment of greatest extremity they looked and saw in the darkness an image in a fluttering robe, walking toward them on the ridges of the sea. They cried out in terror at the sight, thinking that it was a phantom that walked upon the waves. And through the

storm and darkness to them—as so often to us, when, amid the darknesses of life, the ocean seems so great and our little boats so small—there came the ultimate and reassuring voice of peace with this simple declaration, "It is I; be not afraid." Peter exclaimed, "Lord, if it be thou, bid me come unto thee on the water." And Christ's answer to him was the same as to all of us: "Come."

Peter sprang over the vessel's side and into the troubled waves, and while his eyes were fixed upon the Lord, the wind might toss his hair and the spray might drench his robes, but all was well. Only when with wavering faith he removed his glance from the Master to look at the furious waves and the black gulf beneath him, only then did he begin to sink. Again, like most of us, he cried, "Lord, save me." Nor did Jesus fail him. He stretched out his hand and grasped the drowning disciple with the gentle rebuke, "O thou of little faith, why didst thou doubt?"

Then safely aboard their little craft, they saw the wind fall and the crash of the waves become a ripple. Soon they were at their haven, their safe port, where all would one day hope to be. The crew as well as his disciples were filled with deep amazement. . . . [They exclaimed in reverent awe:] "Truly thou art the Son of God." (Adapted from [Frederic W.] Farrar, *The Life of Christ* [Portland, Oreg.: Fountain Publications, 1964], pp. 310–13; see Matt. 14:22–33.)

President Hunter continued:

It is my firm belief that if as individual people, as families, communities, and nations, we could, like Peter, fix our eyes on Jesus, we too might walk triumphantly over "the swelling waves of disbelief" and remain "unterrified amid the rising winds of doubt." But if we turn away our eyes from him in whom we must believe, as it is so easy to do and . . . , if we look to the power and fury of those terrible and destructive elements around us rather than to him who can help and save us, then we shall inevitably sink in a sea of conflict and sorrow and despair. ("The Beacon in the Harbor of Peace," *Ensign,* Nov. 1992, pp. 18–19)

As we pass through the seasons of adversity in our lives, when the rains have lasted so long that the fountains of the deep seem to be broken up and the entire world as we know it is drowning in its despairing depths, may we remember that our task is to do our duty every day with humility and love and courage. May we remain focused on the present moment, acknowledging the sorrow that it may bring but also finding the joy. Let's seize every opportunity we have to lighten up and to see our situation truly, in the light of Christ who is the light of the world. And as we cling to the covenants we have made, may they truly be rainbows of beauty and brilliance to us.

CHAPTER 12

Therefore, Choose Happiness

The concept of choosing happiness is powerful and empowering, because it acknowledges that we are created to experience a fulness of joy, that joy is inextricably involved with our use of agency, and that other things besides happiness will come to us.

Whenever I think of choices, I think of one of my favorite Calvin and Hobbes cartoons. The first frame shows Calvin springing off the school bus. He dashes up the sidewalk exulting, "I'm home! I'm free! The rest of the day is all mine!" He sprints up the front steps grinning broadly and chortling, "Finally, some time to myself! Liberty, precious liberty! Ha, ha, ha!" The last frame of the cartoon shows him slouched in front of the television set, his eyes glazed.

Can we relate to that situation? Do we sometimes find ourselves rejoicing in our freedom but not quite sure what to do with it? Perhaps we're dealing with a universal trait of human nature here, because that's exactly the situation we read about in Deuteronomy when Moses explained the terms of the Lord's covenant to the assembled Israelites in Moab before they entered the promised land. He told them that obedience would bring the blessing of the Lord but disobedience would bring sorrow and lamentations. Then he summarized in the most persuasive way he could:

> See, I have set before thee this day life and good, and death and evil;
>
> In that I command thee this day to love the Lord thy God, to walk in his ways, and to keep his commandments and his statutes and his judgments, that thou mayest live and multiply: and the Lord thy God shall bless thee in the land whither thou goest to possess it.
>
> But if thine heart turn away, so that thou wilt not hear, but shalt be drawn away, and worship other gods, and serve them;
>
> I denounce unto you this day, that ye shall surely perish, and that ye shall not prolong your days upon the land, whither thou passest over Jordan to go to possess it.
>
> I call heaven and earth to record this day against you, that I have set before you life and death, blessing and cursing: therefore choose life, that both thou and thy seed may live:
>
> That thou mayest love the Lord thy God, and that thou mayest obey his voice, and that thou mayest cleave unto him: for he is thy life. (Deuteronomy 30:15–20)

We all know that Moses succeeded in his persuasion; the Israelites accepted the covenant. Sometimes we apologize for the Israelites. We say, "Yes, they accepted the covenant, but then they had a very difficult time living up to its provisions." Or, "Yes, the Lord made them his chosen people, but he had to keep calling them to repentance." I think the "but" doesn't belong in those sentences. We are all human. We all make mistakes. If we didn't, we wouldn't need a Savior and a Redeemer. We are all covenant people; we have all made promises to the Lord; and we all need help living up to those covenants and repenting to maintain our chosenness.

The gospel teaches us to strive for perfection, but we're not expected to reach perfection today or tomorrow. The reason I love the gospel is that it's a system for real people with real problems and real challenges and real conflicts and real joy.

Our happiness doesn't come because we have somehow managed to eliminate all problems, transgressions, and imperfections from our lives; our happiness comes to us mingled with those problems and imperfections. As Father Lehi observed, "It must needs be, that there is an opposition in all things" and "all things must needs be a compound in one." (2 Nephi 2:11.) The way to choose happiness is *not* to choose not to have problems. That system won't work. I once read a saying attributed to Agnes Repplier: "It is not easy to find happiness in ourselves, and it is not possible to find it elsewhere." I don't know anything about Agnes Repplier, besides her name, but I wish I did; I think she is a very wise woman.

I'd like to share two thoughts on how we can choose happiness. First, we must choose prayer, because it is the foundation of our spiritual lives. Without a strong relationship with Heavenly Father and Jesus, it is impossible for us to find true happiness. Second, we must choose kindness as the way in which we lead our lives—but without a spiritual foundation, we simply will not have the strength and will to sustain our desire to be kind.

CHOOSE PRAYER

I would like you to think of prayer as an intense, open communication with our Heavenly Father. Above all, it must be an honest communication. One of my favorite books is *Children's Letters to God,* simply because of the honesty of children's relationships to God. How long has it been since you asked questions like these: "Dear God: How did you know you were God? Charlene." Or here's a letter from a little boy named Tommy: "Dear God, I want to be just like you when I am your age. OK?" (Comp. Eric Marshall and Stuart Hample, enl. ed. [New York: Pocket Books, 1975], n.p.)

We need to have an ongoing conversation with God that shares our whole hearts with him. That means we need to be honest about what we love and what we don't, where we succeed and where we fail, what we're feeling and what we're thinking. One of the most human things about us is the strength and power of our feelings—and some of those feelings are very negative. We feel grief so intensely that we think our hearts will break. We are consumed by a rage so fiery that our whole world seems angry. We feel discouraged. We feel depressed. We aren't always honest, always kind, always faithful. We aren't uniformly cheerful, compassionate, and courageous. And usually it's during those very moments that we choose not to pray, because we think that God doesn't want to see that part of us, respond to such turbulent emotions, or accept us in our negative moments.

I think that the scriptures teach a far different message.

> At the crucifixion, Mary, the mother of Jesus, stood below as the broken body of her son hung from the cross. . . . Mary Magdalene stood weeping at the tomb of Jesus, asking, "If you have carried him away, tell me where you have laid him." (John 20:15). . . . These women, stricken with deep sorrow, went to the place of most intense grief and set themselves in the midst of it. By their actions, they spoke silently

172

to God from the depth of their pain. Their courage in facing their pain enabled them to be comforted by the presence of God. These women teach us an important truth—God can be . . . present to us [only] if are willing to face our pain. . . .

If we are to have an authentic relationship with God, we need to be honest about our pain, our anger and our confusion. If we do not share our pain with God, God cannot comfort us. At first we may feel inhibited in honestly expressing how we feel. Perhaps our religious training has taught us that we cannot be angry or honestly share how we feel with God. We are afraid that God might take offense at our anger, judge our faith-questioning, play down our grief. At times we choose to second-guess God instead of dealing with the pain of our vulnerability.

Certainly the one who created us is aware of our questioning and accepting of our emotions. (Sandra M. Flaherty, *Woman, Why Do You Weep? Spirituality for Survivors of Childhood Sexual Abuse* [New York/Mahwah, N.J.: Paulist Press, 1992], p. 54)

The woman who wrote those words knew exactly what she was talking about. She had been sexually abused by her father for many years during her childhood and then had repressed those negative experiences for many more years. During her thirties, she began having memory flashbacks that finally led to the reconstruction of her abuse. After working through those issues for seven years, she was still struggling with the step of forgiving her father. She acknowledged that, at that point, she could not forgive her father—that forgiveness was simply not in her heart, despite all of her anguished prayers and her hard work in therapy. She writes movingly:

At times my inability to forgive my father confronted me . . . on all levels; the most painful level was the spiritual. I

173

believe that I am a Christian, and I know that one of the basic calls of Christianity is to reconciliation. There were times when I interrogated myself mercilessly, asking how I could stand before God when my heart was filled with hatred. It seemed so basic. I was not debating some theological concept or church teaching. This was Christianity at its core—"love one another."

This was a humbling experience for me. With all my theological training, ideals, and years in [church life], I couldn't forgive him. Even more humbling was the awareness I had in prayer one night. I prayed to God, "I can't do it! I can't forgive him, so you'll have to." Later I let go even further when I prayed, "I'm leaving all of this in your hands. His guilt and my inability to forgive—somehow you will have to take care of it and administer justice."

Then she adds this very important explanation:

I thought if I ever gave up trying to forgive that would prove my guilt. At least if I were trying, there was still a possibility, but [oddly enough] when I gave up and left it in God's hands, I felt free; it was no longer mine. Somehow I have discovered that there is wisdom in the saying, "Put it in God's hands."

I used to think of such statements as pious remarks that made clever bumper sticks but didn't mean much. I believed only passive people would really put it in God's hands. We passionate types wanted part of the action, part of the creating. I used to smile politely at such statements until that moment when there was nothing more that I could do than leave it in God's hands.

It seems so simple, almost too simple. But there are some things which are beyond us. At some point we have to let go and leave the unanswerable questions and conflicts to God. We leave these things in the hands of a God who

174

understands forgiveness, but even more importantly a God who understands justice. (Ibid., pp. 138–39)

In other words, this woman chose happiness. She found peace and acceptance, even in the middle of turmoil and pain, because she was honest and open in her prayer life with our Father in Heaven. She denied nothing of what she was feeling. She didn't try to be sweet. She didn't try to be nice. She was honest, and the Lord could answer her prayers with what she could accept right then. I believe that someday she *will* be able to forgive if she continues her course of honesty.

When we think about commitment to prayer and perseverance in prayer, we often think of Daniel, who refused to cease praying to the true God morning, noon, and night, even when his king, seduced by false counselors, signed a proclamation that meant Daniel's death if he disobeyed it. You know the story of how Daniel persisted in prayer, was denounced by the false counselors, and was brought before the king, who finally realized the foolishness of his actions but still reluctantly ordered that Daniel be cast into the den of lions. You also remember how Daniel prayed, how the king also prayed all night and then hurried to the den of lions to call, with hope but not faith, for Daniel, and how Daniel answered out of the lions' den that he had been preserved by the power and love of his God, who had sent an angel to close the mouths of the lions.

I've often wondered what Daniel said in those prayers offered after the proclamation had been issued, when he knew that he was risking his life in praying. What did he talk with God about? I doubt very much that it was a routine recital about the weather and the success of the missionary program.

No, I think Daniel expressed the feelings of his heart. And what were the petitions of his heart that ascended from that pit? I wish we knew what Daniel said and how he prayed at that time.

We do, however, have record of another prayer that Daniel offered later, after these alarming and dramatic adventures. He had received a vision that he did not completely understand and offered a prayer imploring the Lord's enlightenment. I'm very impressed by how hard he worked to understand the revelation he received and how willingly and graciously God worked to clarify his understanding. Let me read just a few sentences of his wise and humble prayer:

> O my God, incline thine ear, and hear; open thine eyes, and behold our desolations, and the city which is called by thy name: for we do not present our supplications before thee for our righteousnesses, but for thy great mercies. (Daniel 9:18)

Do you understand what he was saying? He was saying, "We do not make requests of you because *we* are righteous, but because of *your* great mercy."

Then, he didn't just sit around and wait for an answer, but he continued "speaking, and praying, and confessing my sin and the sin of my people Israel, and presenting my supplication before the Lord." (Daniel 9:20.) While he was struggling thus in prayer, the Lord sent an angelic messenger to him. The messenger touched him to attract his attention. Daniel says, "And he informed me, and talked with me, and said, O Daniel, I am now come forth to give thee skill and understanding. . . . For thou art greatly beloved: therefore understand the matter, and consider the vision." (Daniel 9:20, 22–23.)

How would you like to have an angel touch you gently and say, "O Chieko (or O Maryanne, or O Harold), I am now come to give thee skill and understanding . . . for thou art greatly beloved: therefore understand the matter, and consider the vision."

We say that we believe that God "will yet reveal many great and important things pertaining to the Kingdom of God." (Article of Faith 9.) Revelation to the Church will come through the prophet, but doesn't that article of faith make you ask questions? What are those great and important things? And who will he reveal them to? Could you be one of those who is struggling to "understand the matter, and consider the vision"? If you are, then you're one of those worthy to receive an angelic visitor. Furthermore, the promise of Joseph Smith to the Nauvoo Relief Society on 28 April 1844 was this: "Angels cannot be restrained from being your associates." (*History of The Church of Jesus Christ of Latter-day Saints*, 2d ed. rev., ed. B. H. Roberts [Salt Lake City: The Church of Jesus Christ of Latter-day Saints, 1932–51], 4:605.) Has this promise come true for you? Both Joseph Smith and Alma promise the ministration of angels to women. Yet such is the respect of our Heavenly Father for our agency that he will very rarely give us something for which we have not asked. What would happen, do you think, if we prayed for revelation, for knowledge, for the comfort of the ministration of angels?

But maybe there's another question rising up to loom over you. Something like this: "Oh, isn't it wrong to pray for such things, or even to think of such things? Aren't these things just for the prophets? Aren't we likely to go astray out of pride or ignorance?" Listen to the words of Moses, when Joshua heard that two men were prophesying in the camp of Israel and cried out to Moses to forbid them. Moses answered, "Would God that all the Lord's people were prophets, and that the Lord would put his spirit upon them!" (Numbers 11:29.) Is it possible that we're asking the wrong questions and limiting the operation of the Holy Ghost, cutting off the spiritual gifts that the Father wants to bestow upon us, and feeling fear rather than faith?

Here's what the Lord himself says:

> For my thoughts are not your thoughts, neither are your ways my ways, saith the Lord.
>
> For as the heavens are higher than the earth, so are my ways higher than your ways, and my thoughts than your thoughts.
>
> For as the rain cometh down, and the snow from heaven, and returneth not thither, but watereth the earth, and maketh it bring forth and bud, that it may give seed to the sower, and bread to the eater:
>
> So shall my word be that goeth forth out of my mouth: it shall not return unto me void, but it shall accomplish that which I please, and it shall prosper in the thing whereto I sent it.
>
> For ye shall go out with joy, and be led forth with peace: the mountains and the hills shall break forth before you into singing, and all the trees of the field shall clap their hands. (Isaiah 55:8–12)

Have you ever heard the hills break into song or the trees clap their hands? To me, this scripture says that the Lord has miracles prepared for us, miracles that we simply can't imagine, marvels that we will never be able to figure out if we try to think of God's thoughts as just variations of our own thoughts.

I have spent a long time discussing prayer for one reason: our happiness in this life depends, I believe, on the quality of our relationship with our Heavenly Father and our Savior; and prayer is the fabric of our relationship with them. Reading the scriptures is thrilling and inspirational because it is the record made by individuals who knew the Savior and testified of his goodness—but it is *their* record, not your record. When we have an honest relationship with the Lord, then we know that he loves us and that we are precious in his sight. That knowledge is what gives us the strength to be sustained during our moments of adversity and trial. And that knowledge of being completely loved by the Savior and by our Father in Heaven is what gives us the desire, the ability, and the will to serve others. When we serve others, then we experience the kind of joy that comes directly from the Savior, who sees us treating others with the compassion and love that he would manifest if he were among us in the flesh.

CHOOSE KINDNESS

If prayer is the foundation and fabric of our whole spiritual life, then kindness is the rest of the building we erect on that foundation and the pattern in the fabric. I think we already understand that. By saying "choose prayer" and then "choose kindness," I'm just putting into other words the Savior's phrasing of the two great commandments: "Thou shalt love the Lord thy God with all thy heart, and with all thy soul, and with all thy mind," and "thou shalt love thy neighbour as thyself." (Matthew 22:37, 39.)

Mother Teresa understands these principles deeply. Of her understanding, someone wrote movingly, "The biggest disease today she says is not leprosy or tuberculosis, but rather the feeling of being unwanted, uncared for and deserted by everybody. The greatest evil is the lack of love and charity, the terrible indifference toward one's neighbour who lives at the roadside assaulted by exploitation, corruption, poverty, and disease." (In Malcolm Muggeridge, *Something Beautiful for God: Mother Teresa of Calcutta* [New York: Walker and Co./Phoenix Press, 1971; large print ed. 1984], p. 68.)

Kindness cannot be calculated, or it is not kindness. I love the Lord's admonition: "Cast thy bread upon the waters: for thou shalt find it after many days." (Ecclesiastes 11:1.) I think we all saw a wonderful example of this principle in the tour the Tabernacle Choir took to Israel. According to the report in the *Ensign*, part of the incredible success they enjoyed in that country came about because of the act of kindness of an unknown usher at the Tabernacle many years earlier:

> Iain B. McKay, director of international media relations for Bonneville Communications, recognized the importance of making the music of the choir available to everyone. Radio and television broadcasts are an important source of music for those living in Israel and the surrounding area. Therefore, Iain's meeting in Jerusalem with Avi Hanani, head of music for the Israel Broadcasting Authority (the umbrella organization for Israeli radio and television, and the Jerusalem Symphony), was a very important event.
>
> "Robert Cundick, Tabernacle organist emeritus, attended the meeting with me," says Brother McKay. "We walked in, and I handed my card to Mr. Hanani. When he saw Salt Lake City on the card he said, 'Let me tell you about Salt Lake City.' "
>
> Mr. Hanani proceeded to tell them about his own experience at Temple Square thirty-two years earlier. During the

summer, his family toured the western United States and stopped at Salt Lake City. A music student, sixteen-year-old Avi got up early the next morning to visit the Tabernacle and hear the Tabernacle Choir's broadcast of "Music and the Spoken Word." When he got there, all the doors were locked, but he could see through a window that the choir was rehearsing. Timidly, he began knocking on each door, and at about the fifth door an usher opened it. Avi simply said, "I am a music student from Jerusalem and I'd like to hear the choir." At that point, the usher could have told the young man to come back later. Instead, he invited him in. The rehearsal stopped, and Richard P. Condie, the conductor of the choir, shook hands with Avi, introduced him to the choir, and invited him to sit in one of the empty choir seats and listen. When the rehearsal ended, someone took Avi to the front row of the Tabernacle, where he sat next to Church officials during the broadcast.

"Mr. Hanani told me, with some emotion, that that was one of his most profound musical experiences as a young man," says Brother McKay. "And then Mr. Hanani asked, 'What can I do for you?' I said that Mayor Teddy Kollek had invited the Tabernacle Choir to come to Israel. Mr. Hanani replied, 'Well, we must have them on Israeli broadcasting.' And I said, 'That's what we're here to discuss.'" This meeting opened the door for the outstanding media support of the Tabernacle Choir's concerts in Israel. . . .

During the choir's tour, both the Berlioz *Requiem* and the a cappella concert performed in the Binyanei Ha'Ooma Convention Center in Jerusalem were broadcast live on the Israel Radio network. Both performances were also recorded by Israel Television for broadcast on a delayed basis. Oren Schindel, head of the director's department at Israel Television, supervised the television coverage. He said, "The word is that whatever Bonneville and the choir want,

the answer is *yes*." (LaRene Gaunt, "One Voice," *Ensign,*
Apr. 1993, p. 46)

Obviously that unknown usher did not know that the sixteen-year-old music student would one day be in a position to
do the Church an immense favor. Nor did the conductor who
invited young Mr. Hanani to sit with the choir during
rehearsals and see that he had a hospitable place during the
performance calculate this kindness, hoping that it would pay
off later. They had the bread of kindness in their hands and
they cast it on the water instead of hoarding it until it became
stale or moldy. And as a result, thousands of Israelis rejoiced
with the choir during its performances, and thousands more
will hear the music as it is rebroadcast.

There's a Japanese proverb, "One kind word can warm
three winter months." I learned this myself from a lovely and
gracious woman, Motoko Yoshimizu Nara. Perhaps you
remember reading an article in the *Ensign* about Fujiya Nara.
Motoko was his wife; and though the article was primarily
about him, I wish that the author had told us more about her.
Perhaps she was harder to write about and understand
because she was a shy woman, totally supportive of her husband, and retiring in the way of traditional Japanese women.
His story was much more exciting—his conversion as a
teenager in 1915, being ordained as the first native Japanese to
become an elder, the long years of isolation when the mission
was closed between 1924 and 1945, and his single-handed
determination to keep the members in touch with each other
and to await the official return of the Church.

I do not know much about Sister Nara's background. I met
her for the first time in 1968 when Ed and I and our two sons

flew to Tokyo from the United States to assume our duties in the newly organized Japan Okinawa Mission. I was forty-two years old, and she was in her late sixties, old enough to be my mother. She was shy and retiring in the way of traditional Japanese women, as I have said, but she was very hospitable, insisting that we come to her home to visit her, which is not usual in traditional Japanese culture.

She knew that we were new to this work, and that I was consumed by questions and doubts. With great tact and sensitivity, she gave me the information that I needed without making me feel inadequate for not already knowing it. She communicated great strength to me by repeating many times, "I am so grateful that you have come to Japan. How marvelous it is that you have come to help establish the Church in Japan and help the Japanese people. How wonderful it is that there will be this new mission. You are an answer to our prayers, and we will pray constantly for your success." She strengthened and steadied me. More than that, by her quiet cheerfulness and her unending generosity she modeled for me how a mission mother could nurture the members and missionaries, strengthening the present and building for the future.

This gracious, very capable woman unobtrusively noticed our needs and quietly met them. In my mind, she is one of the heroines of the Church. When she married Brother Nara, who was just a few weeks short of his twenty-second birthday, Sister Nara had not yet joined the Church, but she willingly participated in a Christian ceremony conducted by Hilton A. Robertson, the mission president. For both of them, the step into Christianity was a step away from the traditional culture of the nation. Theirs was the first Latter-day Saint marriage performed in Japan. The Japan Mission was closed just a few months later, and Sister Nara was not baptized until 1948, twenty-four years later.

During those intervening years, not yet a member, she opened her small apartment home for meetings of the Church and cheerfully welcomed all who came. She must have been frightened often during World War II when Brother Nara was traveling for his job with the railroad—frightened for him in such a vulnerable position and frightened for herself. In fact, their home was destroyed in an air raid in 1945, but they miraculously escaped without injury. The new mission president, Edward L. Clissold, baptized her in April 1948, formally welcoming her into the household of the faith where she had long since earned her place and had, in turn, extended a hospitable and welcoming hand to many, many other Japanese Saints. In many ways, she is the spiritual foremother of what is now a large number of Saints in Japan—and for much of that time, she was not even a member. (See Yukiko Konno, "Fujiya Nara: Twice a Pioneer," *Ensign,* Apr. 1993, pp. 31–33.)

I think of her when I read in Proverbs 31:26: "She openeth her mouth with wisdom; and in her tongue is the law of kindness."

CONCLUSION

We have discussed how happiness can come into our lives through our own choices. We cannot choose not to have problems, but we can choose to be happy by choosing a life that is "after the manner of happiness." (2 Nephi 5:27.) The foundation of that life is prayer to connect us closely to our Heavenly

Father and the Savior, and the rest of the building is the kindly deeds we perform for others, following the Savior's example of serving our brothers and sisters.

Think for a moment of Mother Teresa, of the combination of prayer and kindness in her own life. We all know of her wonderful and loving work among the poor of the Calcutta slums. I have been very drawn to her life. I sense in her a focus and a strength that comes from any disciple who manifests the principles of Christian living in daily life. She says:

> Joy is prayer—Joy is strength. Joy is love. Joy is a net of love by which you can catch souls. God loves a cheerful giver. She gives most who gives with joy. The best way to show our gratitude to God and the people is to accept everything with joy. A joyful heart is the normal result of a heart burning with love. Never let anything so fill you with sorrow as to make you forget the joy of Christ Risen.
>
> We all long for heaven where God is, but we have it in our power to be in heaven with him right now—to be happy with him at this very moment. But being happy with him now means loving as he loves, helping as he helps, giving as he gives, serving as he serves, rescuing as he rescues, being with him twenty-four hours [a day], touching him in his distressing disguise [of poverty, of disease, of illness]. (Muggeridge, *Something Beautiful for God*, pp. 63–64)

One of my favorite scriptures about grace relates directly to the topic of choosing happiness in the gospel. Jacob, the brother of Nephi, tells his listeners that the Lord has not forgotten them, just because they have been led away from the main body of the house of Israel:

> For behold, the Lord God has led away from time to time from the house of Israel, according to his will and pleasure.

185

And now behold, the Lord remembereth all them who have been broken off, wherefore he remembereth us also.

Therefore, cheer up your hearts, and remember that ye are free to act for yourselves—to choose the way of everlasting death or the way of eternal life.

Wherefore, my beloved brethren [and sisters], reconcile yourselves to the will of God, . . . and remember, . . . that it is only in and through the grace of God that ye are saved.

Wherefore, may God raise you from death by the power of the resurrection, and also from everlasting death by the power of the atonement, that ye may be received into the eternal kingdom of God, that ye may praise him through grace divine. (2 Nephi 10:22–25)

May we accept the atonement of Jesus Christ. May we establish a close relationship with him, one that will mean that we will always remember him as he always remembers us. May we choose the happiness that comes from our faith in the Savior and a lifestyle of kindness to others, that we, with Nephi and the Saints of his day, may "praise [the Lord] through grace divine" in the presence of our Heavenly Father.

CHAPTER 13

The Lord of Little Things

One Christmas I read a very thought-provoking article by Alden Thompson, a professor of Old Testament at Walla Walla College. He talked about the terrible reality that we must all face as we grow in the gospel: the phenomenon of the unanswered prayer. For example, Moses prayed for the privilege of entering the promised land to which he had so diligently, and over such a long period of time, led his people. God denied that request, but he gave him a small gift instead: a view of the promised land from a mountaintop. I've wondered about that story. Was Moses satisfied with the glimpse from Mount Pisgah? Did he see the terrible slaughter by which the Israelites would claim their promised land and was he glad not to see his people become violent and cruel? Or did he die unhappy and dissatisfied? Was he hurt? Did he wonder why God refused to reward him as he may have felt he so richly deserved? The scriptures give us no answers to any of those questions.

There are times in all of our lives when we pray desperately, ardently, and faithfully for something and then have to deal with the fact that it doesn't happen. Professor Thompson shares the story of a friend:

"From my childhood," he said, "I have many memories of answered prayers—prayers about lost baseballs or missing pocketknives. But I prayed my most urgent prayer of all when my parents began talking about divorce. I asked God not to let it happen. It happened anyway."

Quietly he added, "I gladly would have given back all those baseballs and pocketknives just to see my parents together."

[Was it] God's will that a marriage fail? Hardly.

[Was it] simply a lack of faith? That would be a cruel burden indeed for a heart already torn by grief. (Alden Thompson, "A God of Little Gifts," *Signs of the Times*, Dec. 1992, p. 29)

Or how about that third answer that we often hear in sermons: God knows what we need better than we do. He gives us what we need, rather than what we want. That is a very unsatisfying answer. Why does a boy "need" divorced parents? Why does he need the shattering of his home and the painful process of reconstituting those personal relationships a bit at a time over the next years, a process so difficult that even as an adult he still feels pain about it? Or take the situation of child sexual abuse. Why does a three-year-old or a six-year-old or a nine-year-old "need" to be raped by a stranger, by a baby-sitter, by a father? Even to ask the question shows that such an answer is not possible from the loving Father in Heaven. When my husband died, many people commented on the rich, righteous, loving life that Ed had lived. The implication was that Ed did not "need" to live longer, that he had accomplished his earthly mission. I knew they meant well, but it was no comfort to me, because *I* needed Ed. I still do. I always will.

Surely part of the healing process in any grief or loss must be to confront God directly with the fact of our need and the seeming lack of an answer. I would not presume to tell anyone else who is struggling with his or her own burden how that process should be working. But may I ask you to consider the possibility that our answer to such questions lies in learning to look, with the eyes of faith, for "little gifts"?

Professor Thompson talks about his own bewilderment at the "mismatch between my wish list and [God's] gift list" but says that being a father has taught him that sometimes he must stifle "the urge to intervene":

> Small gestures and little gifts remind us of a love that longs to help but chooses not to. And all for the greater good. This concern explains the remarkable blend of heroic deliverances and disastrous martyrdoms found in Hebrews 11. All these people of faith wanted something more, and their desire accorded with God's promise, yet they "did not receive what was promised since God had provided something better" (Hebrews 11:39, 40, NRSV). (Ibid.)

That statement requires enormous faith from us. If God gives us a little gift instead of our heart's desire—even when we think it's something we deserve and have earned—can we accept that gift with a thankful heart and see it with the eyes of faith as something that we can rejoice in?

Mother's Day was not a particularly pleasant day for me this year because Ed wasn't there. As I sat through the first part of our sacrament meeting, I was so grateful that I'd been asked to speak in two other meetings and wouldn't have any more time just to sit and think about how alone I felt. I had to leave our meeting a little before it was over to address a group

189

of mothers and daughters in one ward and then go on to a second ward to speak in sacrament meeting.

When I got home, my son Ken, who lives in Salt Lake City, was on the phone. "Hey, Mom, where did you go?" he asked plaintively. "I went to your sacrament meeting because I thought you might be feeling a little lonely, but you left early and disappeared for six hours!" He and I had a good laugh over that. I certainly appreciated his thoughtfulness, but I appreciated more the great blessing that I had been invited to do something for someone else that took my mind off my own troubles.

SEEING OUR LITTLE GIFTS

Let's talk about the ability to see little gifts. The ability to see little gifts is a gift of attitude. For me, it's captured in that wonderful scripture that Jesus gave:

> Are not two sparrows sold for a farthing? and one of them shall not fall on the ground without your Father.
> But the very hairs of your head are all numbered.
> Fear ye not therefore, ye are of more value than many sparrows. (Matthew 10:29–31)

We're all sparrows, neither very important nor irreplaceable in the world's eyes. But God knows each one of us. He sprinkles the crumbs for us to eat. He lets us perch on his fingers. His hands make a safe place for us to nestle down.

With a sparrow attitude, we don't need to beat our beaks against the bakery window. We can feast on crumbs on the window ledge. Each new beginning, each change in our situation, each demand that stretches us in some way is a gift in which we can find something to be thankful for.

Think, for example, of the difference in attitude between these letters written by two little boys. The first boy wrote: "Dear God, I didn't think orange went very good with purple until I saw the sunset you made on Tue. That was cool. Eugene." The second little boy wrote, "Dear God, I just got left back [a grade in school]. Thanks a lot. Raymond." (*Children's Letters to God*, comp. Eric Marshall and Stuart Hample, enl. ed. [New York: Pocket Books, 1975], n.p.)

We might think that Eugene's appreciation is just as natural as Raymond's disappointment, but my point is this: *both* of them are natural reactions. Because of the wonderful gift of agency, we get to choose which attitude will be *our* attitude. We get to choose the sparrow's part, because we choose the sparrow's trust in seeing little gifts.

Here's another example. When I was principal of Holly Hills Elementary School in Denver, I took three of my sixth-graders to compete in the district spelling bee. I knew they would be happy and excited as we went—with some nervousness and worry mixed in—but I wondered what the mood in the car would be when we returned. Would they be disappointed and sad if they didn't win? Would they be discouraged and upset? At day's end my question was answered, and I was so delighted with their maturity. As I feared, not one of the three made it into the finals, but the comments I heard were "I'm so glad I tried out," "We should be happy we made it to this point," and "I'm going to really try again next year." They talked excitedly about being able to choose between pizza and hamburgers for lunch, cheering for the contestants when they spelled the word correctly, feeling terrible with those who didn't spell it right. They participated fully in the experience and had a day to remember. They gave me a day I've never forgotten, either. They were sparrows, grateful for the little gifts. And because they had a sparrow's attitude, they had a wonderful day.

You know the old proverb: "What we must decide is *how* we are valuable rather than how valuable we *are*." We have to respect our own judgments, insights, and opinions and not give them up easily just because someone has a different opinion. "You can't always go by the opinions of the experts all the time," someone has observed. If you were to take an opinion poll about what to stuff a turkey with, what answer would you get from the turkey? A turkey would think the right stuffing consists of "grasshoppers, grit and worms." But if you're doing the stuffing, you get to choose bread crumbs, sage, and onions. (Jo Ann Larsen, "Become Your Own Hero by Boosting Self-Esteem," *Deseret News*, 21 Feb. 1993, S-11.)

How do sparrows stay cheerful? How do they learn to look for the little gifts? It's a great blessing that we can have only one thing in our minds at a time, so when we choose to concentrate on being cheerful—even if we're just fooling ourselves—it usually works for at least a minute or two. I hope we can retain our feeling of being connected to a Heavenly Father and to a Savior who are the Lords of little gifts. I hope we will develop the sparrow's attitude, so that we can see the little gifts that they give us, even when sometimes what we yearn for is a great gift and even when that gift is denied.

BE A GIVER OF LITTLE GIFTS

In addition to developing an attitude of seeing little gifts, we can find a source of immense power in assuring our own happiness by being the kind of person who is a giver of little gifts. Once again, I think that Jesus knows a great deal about being a Lord who gives little gifts, because he probably knew that proverb in Ecclesiastes 11:1: "Cast thy bread upon the waters: for thou shalt find it after many days." Does that make sense? When you don't have any bread to spare, is it reasonable and rational and sensible to cast it on the waters?

I think that in a universe where invisible light streams from the presence of God to fill the immensity of space this proverb makes perfect sense. In a universe where we are all connected through intangible bonds as fragile and as tough as spiderwebs, where something as real as love makes wheels go round and hearts beat and stop, then casting bread on the water makes a lot more sense than storing it on a shelf. Let me tell you some stories about bread-casting.

You may have read a wonderfully thoughtful and appreciative article about the Saints in South Africa in the *Ensign* some time ago. One of the families it talked about was that of Bishop Alan Hogben and his wife, Pauline, of the Sandton Ward in Johannesburg. Soon after they were baptized in 1970, they began talking about attending the temple. "In those days," Bishop Hogben said, "it meant going to London. That represented a financial challenge I felt was impossible to meet."

Nevertheless, they committed themselves to go by applying for their temple recommends. "When the mission president asked us when we planned to go," Bishop Hogben says, "I said that I thought it would be in two and a half years." That was in April 1972. The Hogbens were sealed only five months later, in September.

How on earth could such a thing happen? Well, the Hogbens did their part by setting up a very tight budget that left out all luxuries, but then the windows of heaven started to open for them. "There would come a knock on the door, and someone would bring us a little cake," he said. "For months, we would find a food parcel in the back seat of our car after church. Years later, we found that it came from a sister who knew she could never afford to go to the temple, but by helping us she felt she could participate vicariously in our temple experience."

One evening after sacrament meeting, another member absolutely flabbergasted them by giving them 200 rands. (Right now, the exchange rate is about three rands per dollar.) When the Hogbens asked him why, he said that a stranger had once given his family a gallon of gas when they were stalled. They'd tried to pay him, but he said, "No, just give someone else a gallon when they need it." So that's what this brother was doing.

But the story doesn't stop there. Bishop Hogben said that R200 had "contributed to at least four more couples going to the temple" because "when we returned from the temple, we gave that R200 to another couple, and they gave it to still another. To this day, we don't know how far that R200 went." Bread had floated to them upon the waters of their faith. They had eaten of it gratefully and then cast their own bread upon the water. (R. Val Johnson: "South Africa: Land of Good Hope," *Ensign,* Feb. 1993, p. 38.)

It's the cat's cradle phenomenon—they were able to see, be grateful for, and to celebrate the connections among themselves as brothers and sisters. The elderly sister who slipped food into their backseat was with them in spirit in the temple. The families who received the 200 rands probably did not even know that elderly sister, but because they are part of the Hogbens' spiritual family, they are connected spiritually to her as well. Think of the immense amount of goodwill and love that their little gifts generated. Sisters and brothers, we can do the same thing. Our small gifts may seem insignificant to us, but they are not insignificant to the Lord of little gifts. Think of the great happiness and delight you give him with a kind word, a secret act of helpfulness, a loving gesture.

Let me share with you a personal story about bread I cast on the waters. On March 28, 1993, I spoke at a fireside at Ricks College. (See Chapter 15, "Seek Ye the Best.") I had thought and prayed a great deal about that address because I know that young people are learning so quickly that sometimes they learn things you don't intend, things that may not even be true—and one of the lessons I didn't want them to learn inadvertently is that the gospel is boring! I talked about the five smooth stones that David selected from the brook before he stepped across it and walked out to face Goliath, and I asked the students to consider what their giants were and what some important stones might be to have ready to put in their slings. It was the closing fireside to Ricks's Women's Week, but there were many young men in the audience, and one of them listened to me in the way that every speaker wants to be listened to.

I had a chance to meet him later in Canada where he was home with his family. Before a biregional women's conference that I was to address, I had the opportunity of attending that beautiful temple in Cardston and enjoying a peaceful and inspirational endowment session. When the prayer circle was forming, I waited quietly, thinking of the many times that Ed and I had made a couple in similar circles. And then to my surprise, a very young man, just nineteen or twenty, was leaning over me, whispering, "Sister Okazaki, would you like to come into the prayer circle with me?" I looked up at him with such surprise and delight and whispered, "Oh, thank you very much. I'd be delighted." So I had that experience again—the first time since the death of my husband more than a year before.

He escorted me back to my seat when the prayer was finished, and I gave him a warm hug. Did he have any idea what a great gift he had given me? In the celestial room, I looked until I found him, so that I could learn his name. His name was Brad Crane. I thanked him, but he thanked me over and over. He had heard me speak at Ricks, and then, just a week later, had heard me speak in general conference. Something had made a connection between the two of us so that he felt he could ask me to join him in the prayer circle. And there's no question about it—I have a connection to Brad that will last as long as I have a memory! And I feel connected to his parents, who met me the next day. I could see how proud they were of their fine son, and I shared those feelings as we talked for a few minutes. How grateful I am for the connections in our lives that brought us together—for whatever preparation I had made in giving my talk at Ricks that made it possible for Brad to hear what I was saying, for the training he had received in his family that made it possible for him to offer me such a loving service, and for the bread cast upon the waters of my calling that had returned to me with such love and sensitive generosity in a temple I had never seen before.

Sometimes we feel that the gifts we give are too small to be worth mentioning, and often we don't know the effect our own gifts have. Instead, remember that even a small gift is love made visible. Those little gifts make it easier for us to believe, even in sad or discouraged moments, that we really are upheld in the loving hands of a Father in Heaven who is mindful of every sparrow and who knows the currents of the waters that carry bread away from us and then bring it back again—sometimes with butter and jam on it!

CONCLUSION

I hope that we will not underestimate the little gifts—the little gifts that we receive from God and the little gifts that we can give each other. God prizes little things too. When Alma was passing on to his son Helaman the records that later became the Book of Mormon, he explained that those simple plates were very important, that they had the power to "go forth unto every nation, kindred, tongue, and people, that they shall know of the mysteries contained thereon." (Alma 37:4.) Now, of course, I don't know what Helaman was doing while Alma was explaining this, but it's just remotely possible that he rolled his eyes up and said, "Sure, Dad," because Alma continues in that patient tone of voice that all parents have to develop at some point in their career:

> Now ye may suppose that this is foolishness in me; but behold I say unto you, that by small and simple things are great things brought to pass; and small means in many instances doth confound the wise.
>
> And the Lord God doth work by means to bring about

his great and eternal purposes; and by very small means the Lord doth confound the wise and bringeth about the salvation of many souls. (Alma 37:6–7)

And the Book of Mormon has literally gone forth to "every nation, kindred, tongue, and people," and they have learned "the mysteries contained thereon."

I love Nephi's description of the Liahona in the Book of Mormon, too, because it contains the same idea about the value of little things. Nephi said that the orb of the Liahona contained a

new writing, which was plain to be read, which did give us understanding concerning the ways of the Lord; and it was written and changed from time to time, according to the faith and diligence which we gave unto it. And thus we see that by small means the Lord can bring about great things. (1 Nephi 16:29)

And in our own day, the Lord told Joseph Smith:

Behold, I, the Lord, declare unto you, and my words are sure and shall not fail, that they shall obtain it.

But all things must come to pass in their time.

Wherefore, be not weary in well-doing, for ye are laying the foundation of a great work. And out of small things proceedeth that which is great. (D&C 64:31–33)

This may be a season of sorrow, difficulty, and trial for you. This may be a season when you feel that the demands upon you are great and your resources are few, when you feel as if you are a sparrow whom no one is noticing and as if you are stranded on a shore where no current is passing. Will you please remember that the Savior is the Lord of little things as well as of great things?

See with sparrow eyes—with the eyes of faith. I promise you that the little gifts are there: the sunsets that are orange and purple, the choice between hamburgers and pizza, the son who slips into your Mother's Day program. And the second important part is to practice bread-casting—to see what we ourselves can give to others. They may look very small to us—these gifts that we pass on—but they are not small to the Lord, and we have no way of knowing how far they may extend into the lives of others.

As Mother Teresa says, "We can do no great thing—only little things with great love." (*Love: A Fruit Always in Season: Daily Meditations from the Words of Mother Teresa Calcutta*, ed. Dorothy S. Hunt [San Francisco, Calif.: Ignatius Press, 1987], p. 121.) I pray that we may all have the experience of knowing that we are part of the great work of our loving Heavenly Father, that through us he is doing his great work of bringing to pass the immortality and eternal life of every living being.

Pressing
Forward

CHAPTER 14

Banzai to Bonsai:
Some Thoughts for Young People

I want to teach you two Japanese words. The first one is *banzai*. It means, roughly, "hooray!" or "terrific!" The second Japanese word I want to teach you sounds a little bit like the first one. It's *bonsai*. It refers to the miniature trees that are such a historic art form in Japan.

PATIENCE

Creating a bonsai requires great patience. The word in Japanese means "tray planting" or "tree in a pot." The art of creating miniature rock and plant gardens was developed twenty centuries ago in China by Buddhist monks who revered these tiny trees as symbols linking the divine to human nature. So at approximately the same time Christ was born in Palestine, the art of bonsai was developing in China, and it was introduced to Japan in the tenth or the eleventh century. Bonsai is a "living art form." That means it "is the painting which is never finished, the sculpture never quite complete." (Bernie Ward, "Perfect Proportions," *Sky*, Dec. 1992, p. 30.)

Common forms of bonsai are junipers, redwoods, pines, cypresses, maples, oaks, and apples. There are no special dwarf bonsai species or miniature species. They are all trees that would grow eighty or a hundred feet high in the forest. But "in bonsai, [they are] measured—and treasured in inches and centimeters." (Ibid.) These trees are enchanting, mysterious. Unless there is something next to them, you have to blink hard to see what proportions they really have.

The perfect bonsai is a perfect tree, just in a pot instead of in the earth. I read about a ponderosa pine that was selected for bonsai in 1964 from a parent tree more than six hundred years old. That little shoot carries all of the characteristics of a ponderosa pine in it. That's why as an exquisite bonsai it looks exactly like a ponderosa in miniature.

Like the bonsai trees, we are miniatures of something greater. We are children of God. We get to practice, in our own little pots and our own pocket gardens, all of the traits of our Heavenly Father: love, service, wisdom, justice, mercy, faith, knowledge, diligence . . . you name it. We can practice it. God is perfect in his galaxy. We can be perfect in our pots.

But of course, practice requires patience. I'm glad for the chance to practice in patience. The apostle Paul wrote to the Thessalonians that he remembered "your work of faith, and labour of love, and patience of hope in our Lord Jesus Christ, in the sight of God and our Father." (1 Thessalonians 1:3.) Patience *is* a hopeful characteristic. It means that there is something worth working for, worth enduring for.

God's patience with us means that we have all the time we need, as long as we're trying. We can start over as many times as we need. Life isn't a race. God isn't waiting at some mythical finishing line, tapping his foot, glancing at his stopwatch, and muttering, "Hey, get a move on, will you?" As long as we're moving in the direction of sainthood and are sincerely trying, he's happy. In fact, far from waiting at the finishing line, he's there, right beside us, encouraging us and sometimes even lifting us over the rough spots.

And we can be the same way with our lives. We can be patient with ourselves in accomplishing our goals. Let me tell you about Laurel Thatcher Ulrich. She's the third Latter-day Saint and the first Latter-day Saint woman ever to win the Pulitzer prize for history. She won it for her book, *A Midwife's Tale: The Life of Martha Ballard*. The Pulitzer prizes are awarded in various categories of popular writing, but Laurel also won the Bancroft Prize, which is the professional historians' award recognizing "outstanding scholarship. Not since 1963 had a woman won it." (Eugene England, "The Pulitzer: Laurel Thatcher Ulrich," *This People*, Summer 1991, p. 19.) She also won the Joan Kelly and John H. Dunning Prizes of the American Historical Association, which means that her historical colleagues in America looked at her book and at her work and decided it was simply the best that had been done. And then, as if this weren't enough, Laurel also won the megaprize, the prestigious MacArthur Award that brings with it a no-strings-attached prize of three hundred twenty thousand dollars to be used in any way she wants. Now, there's somebody who deserves at least three banzais.

Laurel is a wonderful example of patience. Her book was, as Paul said, a "labour of love" in the "patience of hope." Three decades ago, she was the student commencement speaker at her graduation from the University of Utah, and on 12 June 1992 she returned to the University of Utah to give the commencement address:

I am grateful that 32 years ago, I earned both a Phi Beta Kappa key and a safety pin, and that for the past twenty years I have been able to combine motherhood with "a practical life-work." My children's lives have been enriched by my scholarship, and my scholarship has been enriched by my life as a housewife and mother. When people ask me how I have done it, I usually say, "A little at a time." ("A Phi Beta Kappa Key and a Safety Pin," *Exponent II*, vol. 17, no. 1, p. 19)

Now, pay attention to that. Laurel smiled when she said it, and so did most of the women in the audience. I think it's great to do things a little at a time when you're giving your time to other things that are important to you, such as your family and your church responsibilities. Laurel repeatedly put these obligations first while pursuing an advanced degree, and she chose not to work outside the home while her children were young. Though she writes best in the early morning hours, she gave up that time for a number of years to teach early-morning seminary. Laurel says: "It took me five years to complete a one year M.A., nine to do a Ph.D., eight years to write Martha Ballard's book. Meanwhile Gael and I *together* raised our [five] children." (Ibid.)

Another reason Laurel is a good example of patience is that she discovered only gradually her great love, shifting from English to history and beginning to ask questions about the lives of colonial women. Sometimes when we are young, we dream many dreams, pursue many rainbows, and try many directions. Sometimes that's a necessary stage of experimentation until we discover what brightens our eyes and makes us wake up happy for each new day. Sometimes it's a frustrating stage when we look back on all the new directions we've tried and wonder if we've just been going around in a circle. Be patient with your own dreams when you discover that you have competing demands on your time that mean you need to do things a little at a time. Most women have the opportunity to marry and to raise children. For both young men and young women, partnership with a spouse and parenting of the children who come to bless your home will come first. I hope for each one of you that your marriage is happy and successful, that parenthood is deeply satisfying, and that you fall in love with your life's work, whether that involves paid employment or not.

If it seems to take a long time to discover it, or if you have more love than time to pursue it for a while, be patient. Think of Laurel's patient discovery of her own scholarly love. Think of how patiently she worked on the Martha Ballard project. She was willing to spend years on it, a little bit at a time. You can do the same.

Maren Mouritsen, assistant vice president and dean of student life at Brigham Young University, said these thrilling words during the opening session of one BYU Women's Conference: "To never brace for the supreme effort, to never be all you can be, is a personal tragedy. To never reach one's true stature or capacity is the misuse of our greatest resource, the human resource." ("There's a Horse in the House," *BYU Today,* July 1992, p. 42.)

Don't give up on your dreams. Instead, think of the bonsai, slowly growing year by year toward its perfect shape. Think of Laurel, finding room in her life for both the safety pin and the Phi Beta Kappa pin, and patiently working away at recovering the voice of Martha Ballard. Think of Heavenly

Father's patience with us, and then be a little patient with yourself when you find yourself making a mistake. Be a little patient with yourself when you can't achieve all that you want to by Tuesday. Be a little patient with your parents and your brothers and sisters when you feel that you're the most misunderstood teenager in the entire western world. Have you seen that poster that reads: "Be patient. God isn't finished with me yet!" Let's hear it for patience. Banzai! Banzai! Banzai!

DISCIPLINE

Now let's look at the second characteristic of the bonsai—discipline. It takes a lot of effort to make a bonsai. There's no such thing as a "natural" bonsai. Each one has to be created by hand. The bonsai artist needs to prune the tree carefully, always visualizing the end product. It is potted and repotted many times. The branches are carefully wrapped and wired to create just enough tension to shape the tree so that it leans in a particular way. The roots are also pruned.

Yet all of this shaping does not reduce the tree's natural vitality. These trees are not limited or diminished. "A healthy bonsai is as vigorously alive as its full grown counterpart." (Ward, "Perfect Proportions," p. 30.) There are bonsai in the Japanese Imperial collection that are more than five hundred years old. That means these trees were alive and loved and growing toward their perfect shapes when Columbus was sailing across the Atlantic.

When a tree is being shaped, it's called being in training. We also are in training—in training for godhood. We talked earlier about how we can consider ourselves as little bonsai with the capacity for the perfection of its huge counterpart in the forest. We have the characteristics of God within us because we are his children.

Discipline isn't a word that occurs very often in the scriptures—only once, I think, and then not in the sense that we normally use it. Rather, the scriptural equivalent of the term is *steadfastness* or *persistence.* And the scriptures *do* have quite a bit to say about steadfastness. Nephi talked about steadfastness in Christ in three different places in almost the same words. In 2 Nephi 25:24, he said, "We . . . look forward with steadfastness unto Christ, until the law shall be fulfilled." In 2 Nephi 26:8, he said, "Behold, the righteous . . . hearken unto the words of the prophets, and . . . look forward unto Christ with steadfastness." And then there's this lovely scripture in 2 Nephi 31: "Wherefore, ye must press forward with a steadfastness in Christ, having a perfect brightness of hope, and a love of God and of all [people]. Wherefore, if ye shall press forward, feasting upon the word of Christ, and endure to the end, behold, thus saith the Father: Ye shall have eternal life." (2 Nephi 31:20.) In our own day, the Lord counseled us through Joseph Smith: "Wherefore, be not deceived, but continue in steadfastness" (D&C 49:23) and "For even yet the kingdom is yours, and shall be forever, if you fall not from your steadfastness. Even so. Amen" (D&C 82:24.)

Now, steadfastness is not a terribly glamorous or flashy quality. Discipline is very seldom dashing or romantic, even though the results can sometimes be very dramatic. People all over the world were cheering when Utah's Missy Marlow performed her gymnastic routines at the Olympics. But there weren't any cheering crowds during those hours and hours of preparation while she was learning exactly when to stiffen her wrists or exactly how to point a toe.

What in your life calls out for steadfastness? for consistency in purpose? for discipline in expecting high standards of yourself day in and day out? Maybe it's as mundane as sitting down with your homework every day after school, no matter what's going on outside—falling leaves, falling snow, or falling apple blossoms. Maybe it's getting up from the dinner table and taking your dishes to the sink, and then coming back to carry another load away from the table. Maybe it's as simple as speaking gently to your younger brothers and sisters instead of snarling at them, or speaking respectfully to your parents. Maybe it's as straightforward and uncomplicated as kneeling down for prayer morning and night. Daniel probably didn't think he was doing anything spectacular in the mere fact of his praying, but it became literally a death-defying act.

I want to make another point about discipline. We usually think about it as future-oriented. I imagine you hear a lot about preparation—preparing for a mission, preparing for college, preparing for marriage. Am I right? Well, I want you also to see discipline as something that's now-centered. Daniel wasn't praying every day thinking, "Oh boy, oh boy, am I ever going to stop those lions cold when I get thrown in the den five years from now." No, he was enjoying the relationship that he had with God right then, that day, that minute. You can participate in a family home evening discussion not because it's good training for debating an investigator into submission when you're on your mission but because it's fun to exchange ideas and to learn what other people are thinking.

It's great to have goals. It's terrific to plan on missions, young women as well as young men, to look forward to college or to taking up a vocation, to anticipate marriage and parenthood. Those are wonderful pictures that we paint of a future. By loving those pictures in advance, we make them come true for us. But living only for results and putting all of our energy into our goals sometimes means that we can miss living in the present.

As you may know, one of my favorite books is *Children's Letters to God*, very short, one-sentence letters written by grade-school children. Some of them have more sincerity, I think, than many of the longest prayers we hear. One of those letters is from a little girl who wrote, "Dear God, When you make a miracle everybody says it is great, but I can't even play a trick without getting it. Allison," and in another a little boy asks, "Dear God, What is the use of being good if nobody knows it? Mark." (*Children's Letters to God*, comp. Eric Marshall and Stuart Hample, enl. ed. [New York: Pocket Books, 1975], n.p.) In both of these letters, the children are dealing with the question of being results-centered.

What *is* the use of being good if nobody knows it? Well, in the first place, you know and I know that somebody *does* know it. You know it. God knows it. But even more important, those cumulative choices for good, made hour by hour and day piled on day, mean that you're becoming the kind of person who embodies and personifies goodness. But that's in the future. Most important of all is the right now, at that moment of being good when nobody knows it. Even if it causes you some social dissonance, you can have a sense of harmony with the goodness of the universe and the satisfaction of knowing who you are. You know that the difference between a miracle and a trick isn't just a matter of being caught.

Another point about discipline I want to stress is this. We usually think of discipline as the ability to say no. No to drugs. No to premarital sex. No to certain movies and TV shows. Part of that is true. But also think of discipline as the ability to say yes.

A friend gave me this little essay of encouragement by a writer named Jim Vandenberg. Think about the discipline required to follow its advice:

> People can be unreasonable, illogical, and self-centered—but love them anyway.
>
> Do good for others, and your motives will be suspect, but do it anyway.
>
> Small [people] with big ideas can be discouraged by big [people] with small minds—but think big anyway.
>
> Give the best you have to give and people will find fault—but give your best anyway.
>
> What you spend years building may be destroyed overnight by well-meaning, thoughtless people, but build anyway.
>
> If you are successful, you will win false friends and true adversaries, but succeed anyway.
>
> The good you do today may be forgotten tomorrow but do good anyway. ("Anyway," column from unidentified publication, April 1991, n.p.; photocopy in my possession)

The bonsai represents the simplicity and beauty achieved by constant discipline. Think of holding an entire landscape in your hand! So let's hear it for discipline. Banzai! Banzai! Banzai!

LOVE

I read a wonderful statement by a bonsai artist speaking about a tree. He said: "Bonsai artists invest in their trees the way parents invest in their children's future. We see every inch of these trees. We take them out of their pots. We periodically wash and trim the roots. We bend and train the branches and do maintenance grooming. It's an intimate relationship—much more intimate than simply growing a geranium in a pot." (Ward, "Perfect Proportions," p. 38.) He also described the thrill of seeing the tiny tree do exactly what larger trees do. In the autumn, the tiny leaves of a deciduous tree turn yellow and fall to the ground. In spring, the bonsai apple tree turns pink and white with blossoms. In the fall its exquisite little apples turn scarlet.

This bonsai master compared the loving feelings of the artist for his or her tree to the love of a parent for a child. Most of you [seminary students] have quite properly decided to postpone becoming parents for a few years, but I believe that you already know quite a lot about love. I think probably most of you feel a great deal of love for your parents—at least most of the time. Take on trust my promise and your parents' promise that you'll learn about an even more wonderful love when you marry, and a love more wonderful still when you become parents. Have the patience and the discipline to love as God loves—without cheating, without self-indulgence.

CONCLUSION

Remember the lesson of the bonsai, a living creation, a miniature masterpiece that is practicing perfection. We, in the limited sphere called mortality, are the children of God, in training for godhood. In our earthenware pots and lava rocks, we can strive for the perfection of God in his glorious galaxy and heavenly courts.

Being perfect doesn't mean we've accomplished everything. It means we are making progress along the right path. Just like the bonsai artist, we can practice patience with our own growth, being gentle with ourselves as we try and fail and try again. We can lighten up on ourselves when we make mistakes, when our families can't read our lips, let alone our minds, and when everything around us seems dark. We can exercise the discipline of being steadfast, saying yes to good things as well as saying no to things not quite so good, and enjoying living in the present as well as preparing for the future. And third, we can see love in the pattern of our lives. In our comings together and our separatings, in the points of connection and in the spaces between us, let us recognize the love of Christ. I testify to you that our Heavenly Father has his hand upon you, that he knows you, that he loves you, that he is saying, "You are mine."

CHAPTER 15

Seek Ye the Best

The concept "seek ye the best" echoes two powerful scriptures. The first is from Doctrine and Covenants 88, verse 118: "And as all have not faith, seek ye diligently and teach one another words of wisdom; yea, seek ye out of the best books words of wisdom; seek learning, even by study and also by faith." The second scripture is "Choose you this day whom ye will serve; . . . but as for me and my house, we will serve the Lord." (Joshua 24:15.)

I want to share some thoughts about seeking the best, and I want to do it with the example of a young person who can be a model for all of us. The person I'm thinking of is David, who was quite young at the time he slew the giant Goliath. The Bible (see 1 Samuel 17:1–51) tells us that the Philistines gathered their forces for war and Saul and the Israelites drew up their forces to meet them. The Philistines occupied one hill and the Israelites another, with a valley between them. A champion named Goliath, who was from Gath, came out of the Philistine camp. He was more than nine feet tall. He had a bronze helmet on his head and wore a coat of bronze armor weighing about one hundred twenty-five pounds; on his legs he wore greaves, and a javelin was slung on his back. His spear shaft was like a "weaver's beam"; its iron point weighed about thirty pounds. His shield bearer went ahead of him.

Goliath stood and shouted to the ranks of Israel, "Choose you a man for you, and let him come down to me. If he be able to fight with me, and kill me, then will we be your servants: but if I prevail against him, and kill him, then shall ye be our servants, and serve us." Then the Philistine said, "I defy the armies of Israel this day." On hearing the Philistine's words, Saul and all the Israelites were dismayed and terrified.

You can imagine how demoralizing it was to have had this spectacle and defiance going on for forty days, twice a day, by the time David arrived in camp with food for his brothers. He reached the camp just as the men were assembling in their battle lines—although we don't know whether it was the evening or the morning roll call. He left his supplies with the officer and ran to the battle lines, where he greeted his three brothers. Then Goliath shouted his usual defiance, and David heard it. When the Israelites ran from him in great fear, David asked, "Who is this uncircumcised Philistine, that he should defy the armies of the living God?"

David's words were overheard and reported to Saul, who sent for him. David said to Saul, "Let no [one's] heart fail because of him; thy servant will go and fight with this Philistine."

Saul replied, "Thou art not able to go against this Philistine to fight with him: for thou art but a youth, and he a man of war from his youth."

But David bore a strong testimony to him that he had defended his father's flocks from bears and lions and affirmed, "The Lord that delivered me out of the paw of the lion, and out of the paw of the bear, he will deliver me out of the hand of this Philistine."

Saul replied, "Go, and the Lord be with thee." Then Saul dressed David in his own armor, and David fastened on his sword. When he tried walking around, he said to Saul, "I cannot go with these; for I have not proved them." Then he removed Saul's armor, took his staff in his hand, chose five smooth stones from the stream, put them in his shepherd's bag, and, with his sling in his hand, approached the Philistine.

Goliath looked David over and "disdained him: for he was but a youth, and ruddy, and of a fair countenance. And the Philistine said unto David, Am I a dog, that thou comest to me with staves? And the Philistine cursed David by his gods. . . . Come to me, and I will give thy flesh unto the fowls of the air, and to the beasts of the field.

"Then said David to the Philistine, Thou comest to me with a sword, and with a spear, and with a shield: but I come to thee in the name of the Lord of hosts, the God of the armies of Israel, whom thou hast defied.

"This day will the Lord deliver thee into mine hand; and I will smite thee, and take thine head from thee; and I will give the carcases of the host of the Philistines this day unto the fowls of the air, and to the wild beasts of the earth; that all the earth may know that there is a God in Israel.

"And all this assembly shall know that the Lord saveth not with sword and spear: for the battle is the Lord's, and he will give you into our hands."

As the Philistine moved closer to attack, David ran to meet him. Reaching into his bag and taking out a stone, he slung it and struck the Philistine on the forehead. The stone sank into his forehead, and he fell to the ground.

"So David prevailed over the Philistine with a sling and with a stone." Then David took Goliath's own sword and cut off his head.

Put yourself in David's place as he faces the giant, a giant that very possibly could vanquish him, a giant that has vanquished many other valiant fighters, and one that is awesomely equipped to do battle. In fact, everyone who knows about this giant communicates the dubious message, "Gee, that's a pretty big giant out there. Are you out of your mind?"

Put yourself in David's position, too, as he realizes that even the king's armor will be no protection and that he must face the giant with the weapons he already knows best. Think about David, kneeling at the stream that runs through the bottom of the valley where the two armies are drawn up. He knows his life might depend on the stones that he selects. What does he look for? I've never used a sling in my life, so I have to imagine this part with you, but I'm sure he considered size and weight and shape. What is the precise point of balance between a stone that is heavy enough to do the job and one that is so heavy he wouldn't be able to throw it properly? How big does the stone need to be? What shape fits best into his sling?

As David bent over the streambed, running his eye over the stones lying on its bottom, I'm sure he was concerned to choose the best. His life depended on his choice, after all.

Think about his seeking and his choosing. David selected *five* stones, not one. It took only one, as matters turned out, and he had no way of knowing whether he would have time to hurl more than one, but he had four more in his pouch, just in case.

Now, I'd like to apply this situation to all of us, as if we were David kneeling beside the streambed with Goliath lumbering down the hill toward him, bellowing insults and threats. You need to choose five smooth stones. Which ones will they be? Which ones will make an effective weapon against your giant?

Perhaps for you the giant is chronic ill health and your body itself is something of an enemy to you. Perhaps it is poverty, and you are engaged in hand-to-hand combat with a lack of financial resources as you struggle to gain your education. Perhaps it is being the only member of the Church in your family and dealing with the misunderstandings and pressures from loved ones who don't accept your decision. Perhaps it is loneliness and feelings of isolation. Perhaps it is struggling to heal from physical, emotional, or sexual abuse. Whatever your giant may be, it always brings with it severe doubts about your own ability to cope. There's nothing like a giant to make you feel little and scared.

You get to pick your stones yourself, because only you know your giant and only you know your sling; but my suggestions would be these five: First, get the very best education you can; second, choose the best mentors and models that you can; third, be patient as you work toward your goal; fourth, have faith in Christ; and fifth, have faith in yourself.

CHOOSE THE BEST EDUCATION

First, obtain the very best education you can. The scriptures tell us to "seek learning even by study, and also by faith, as thou hast said . . . that they may grow up in thee, and receive a fulness of the Holy Ghost, and be organized according to thy laws, and be prepared to obtain every needful thing." (D&C 109:14–15.)

David may not have had an opportunity to learn mathematics and German, but he had the very best education possible for killing giants. He'd spent a lot of time in a hazardous environment containing such four-footed giants as bears and lions. He was very motivated to protect the helpless sheep against these giants. He thus brought a combination of love and skill to his encounter with Goliath. He knew which stones to select, because he had selected dozens and hundreds and thousands of stones and had spent hundreds of hours honing his education in how to use a sling before he ever encountered the giant. I don't think he would have been anywhere near as effective if he'd tried to fight in borrowed armor. He couldn't even move in it effectively. Nor would he have been anywhere near as effective if he'd been saying, "Oh yes, a sling. Now, which end do you hold? And where do you put the stone?" He'd been educated *before* he met his giant.

It's important to think, but it's also important to learn how to think. Let me illustrate with an example based on this seemingly innocent vegetable—the carrot. Did you know that carrots can be hazardous to your health? Just listen to these killer statistics:

> Nearly all sick people have eaten carrots. Obviously, the effects are cumulative.
>
> An estimated 99.9 percent of all people who die from cancer and ruptured appendix have eaten carrots.
>
> Another 99.9 percent of people involved in auto accidents ate carrots within 60 days of the incident.

Some 93.1 percent of gang members come from homes where carrots were frequently served.

Among the people born in 1839 who later dined on carrots, there has been a 100 percent mortality rate.

Studies have shown, based on recent laboratory tests, that rats who were fed 500 pounds of carrots per day died within 3 weeks.

Many bunnies have been examined post-mortem and were found to have eaten carrots.

All surviving carrot eaters born between 1900 and 1910 have wrinkled skin, brittle bones, few if any of their own teeth, and failing eyesight.

Virtually all people who experience depression for at least 45 minutes a week are known to have eaten carrots sometime during their life. (*Hope Healthletter* 12 [January 1992]: 1)

Have I made my point? Every one of those statistics is factually accurate, but each one sets up a false cause and effect relationship. If you learn the facts but don't learn how to think about the facts, you'll be vulnerable to people who come along and try to scare you about carrots.

I've been a teacher for most of my adult life. There are few things I care about as passionately as I do about education. (The gospel happens to be one, and my family happens to be another—and in this I suspect I'm very much like you.) I have a great deal of faith in the *process* of education. As human beings, we have a joy and a delight in learning built into our very cells and bones because a hunger for knowledge is part of our spirits. We came from the premortal existence having chosen a path where choice was guaranteed and inescapable. We wanted to find out for ourselves, experience for ourselves, understand for ourselves, and give a free and loving allegiance to our Savior.

The path of fear, of conformity, and of safety was Satan's path, and we rejected that. To me that means that we can have a lot of confidence in our ability to make correct decisions as long as our hearts do not waver in their first allegiance to Christ. The college years are a wonderful time to explore many subjects, many approaches, many theories, and many philosophies. It's the right time to be asking yourself, "What do I really think about that? How do I really feel about this?"

CHOOSE THE BEST MENTORS AND MODELS

If the first step is to get the best education we can, then the second is to choose the best mentors and models possible. We don't know who taught David to use a sling. Possibly it was his father. Possibly it was his older brothers. We also don't know who taught David his faith in the Lord. We know nothing of his mother, but perhaps she had something to do with it. One of my favorite passages from the Book of Mormon describes the importance of choosing good examples to follow. The Savior says:

> Verily, verily, I say unto you, this is my gospel; and ye know the things that ye must do in my church; for the works which ye have seen me do that shall ye also do; for that which ye have seen me do even that shall ye do;
>
> Therefore, if ye do these things blessed are ye, for ye shall be lifted up at the last day. (3 Nephi 27:21–22)

Who are your mentors? One of my most important models was a woman I encountered when I was an elementary-school student, living in my little village of Mahukona on the big island of Hawaii. The sixth-grade teacher in our little school was Yuriko Yamamoto Nishimoto. She was the first person I knew who had gone to college from our area and who had come back. She gave me the courage to dream the same dream about myself. Up to that point, I thought that only Caucasians could really become somebody; they were the people who ran our plantation. The Japanese and the Hawaiian people were the laborers. Even as a tiny child, I knew the difference between the so-called important people and my own family. Most of the other teachers were Caucasian. But Mrs. Nishimoto gave me an incentive. I could see myself in her.

I resolved to get an education and become a teacher myself. This resolve was tested when I was fifteen. The gasoline rationing imposed during World War II meant that the school buses could no longer take the high school students every day to Honomakau, ten or twelve miles away. My parents and I decided that I was old enough to leave home, go to Honomakau, and work as a maid for my room and board. I worked for Mr. and Mrs. Ehrlich, who both taught school in Kohala. They lived in a duplex, and in the other half of the duplex was Mrs. Nishimoto who, by then, was teaching business education at the high school.

Nearly all of the teachers were very kind to me, knew my circumstances, and took an interest in me. They all tried to help me as much as they could. But Mrs. Nishimoto was especially kind. I used to visit her often and share with her some of the ideas and questions I had that my mother was too far away to answer. She took me under her wing in a way. Once, when the question of the junior prom came up, Mrs.

Nishimoto, who knew the circumstances of my family and my distance from my mother, said, "I'll make a formal for you." I was stunned at her generosity and kindness. She painstakingly sewed a beautiful green and lavender gown in a light, floating cotton with a bolero jacket. I can still see how it flared and remember how elegant I felt in it. It was so nice that I even took it to the university and used it there. Mrs. Nishimoto became my mentor not only in terms of my dream to get an education but also in terms of her kind and generous heart.

I remember reading a very interesting article by Greg Palmer called, "Everything I Really Needed to Know I Learned at Ricks College." I don't know Brother Palmer personally, but the biographical note identified him as a director of the LDS Foundation and a Book of Mormon teacher at Ricks College. He talked about many lessons he had learned at Ricks College, but one of his examples stood out. He describes Dr. Lyle Lowder, who taught him anatomy and physiology with impressive learning, and then says:

> But what I remember most vividly was something else. With the vigor characteristic of this man who so deeply felt what he taught, he spoke to us of Guatemala and the deprivation and struggles he'd seen there. He spoke, too, of the sacrifices of some students to attend Ricks. Then came a completely appropriate tirade—don't waste paper hand towels. Use one, then flail your hands in the air a bit and use the evaporative process God set up on this earth! If we each would save just a few paper towels a day we would have enough money to enable Guatemalans to eat properly and be inoculated, or provide scholarships for those who couldn't afford school!
>
> For fourteen years since then, I've walked down unnumbered halls with hands dripping.

The point is not just a few paper towels. It is about being wise with the resources God has given us, and it is about doing without frills so someone else can have necessities.

How I admire the recyclers, the gardeners, the patchers, the salvagers, those who don't walk on the grass, the wise stewards.

Our throwaway culture can be horrifying, where we without so much as a sideways glance so readily dispose of our shaving razors and beverage containers and last season's wardrobes.

And people. (*This People,* Fall 1992, pp. 31–33)

Dr. Lowder was a mentor for Greg Palmer. I suspect that Brother Palmer has become a mentor himself for many others. I encourage you to look for models, find them, and follow them. But remember that mentors and models have their limitations, too. This point is made in an irresistible way in one of my favorite books, in which children, probably in the second and third grade, described their perceptions of fathers. One little boy named Jeff wrote: "You go to a Father when your in a spot. He gives you some advice and sometimes it can get you into trouble. A father is a help at everything but there's one thing you have to be careful of he's not always wright." Another little boy named John wrote: "Ask father how to spell conscience and he says you look it up." (*What Is a Father? Children's Responses,* comp. Lee Parr McGrath and Joan Scobey [New York: Simon & Schuster, 1969], n.p.)

Remember that even mentors and models get to make mistakes, too. They're human, just as we are. And the best mentors and models are like John's father, even though John sounds a little crabby about it. They give you tools and teach you how to use them, and then they actually *make* you use them. The best mentors don't want groupies or disciples. They want a new generation of scholars and Christians who can stand on their own and become mentors to another generation.

So these are two of our stones: get the best education you can, and seek the best mentors and models you can.

BE PATIENT

The third stone is to be patient as you work toward your goal. Paul's epistle to the Hebrews cautions new Saints: "For ye have need of patience, that, after ye have done the will of God, ye might receive the promise." (Hebrews 10:36.) We don't know whether David was a patient or an impatient person. If we look at his later life and read the story of Bathsheba, we suspect that there were moments when he had no patience at all. But we also need to look at the long years when King Saul was slowly going mad and became convinced that David was his enemy. David spent many years in the wilderness, hiding from Saul, refusing to attack him when provoked, and even refusing to take revenge on him when Saul was asleep and helpless in his presence. So David was probably like most of us. He had moments of impatience and self-indulgence, but he also had moments of great patience and forbearance. Perhaps part of that patience was learned out with the sheep on those long, slow, hot afternoons. Perhaps some of that patience came as he hurled stones at a mark, patiently improving a little bit each day until he could hit the target right in the middle.

What if David had become impatient with himself because he missed the target the first three times he tried? What if he had thrown down his sling and walked away in disgust? What if he had felt very depressed because he wasn't doing as well as he thought he should and refused to try any more? The bear and the lion would have enjoyed a much tastier meal than they got and Goliath would have had things his own way on the field of battle.

Jo Ann Larsen, a columnist in the *Deseret News*, encourages people to give themselves "lots of room to make mistakes. Gobs and gobs of room, as a matter of fact. Every one of the 5 billion people on this planet makes several mistakes a day, so don't make yourself a 'Special Case'—a person who can't make a mistake without penalty. Be like Thomas Edison who, when someone asked him why he persisted when he had already failed 9,000 times, replied, 'I haven't even failed once; nine thousand times I've learned what doesn't work.'" ("Become Your Own Hero by Boosting Self-Esteem," *Deseret News*, 21 Feb. 1993, S-11.)

HAVE FAITH IN CHRIST

The fourth stone with which to attack your giant is to have faith in Christ. In importance, this stone undoubtedly should come first. Remember how David expressed his astonishment at Goliath's challenge? He said, "Who is this uncircumcised Philistine, that he should defy the armies of the *living* God?" (1 Samuel 17:26; emphasis added.)

Is our God a living God? I just love a book I have of children's letters to God. One is from a little boy, probably in the first or second grade, who wrote, "Dear Mr. God, How do you feel about people who don't believe in you?" Then he added quickly, "Somebody else wants to know. A friend, Neil."

(*Children's Letters to God,* comp. Eric Marshall and Stuart Hample, enl. ed. [New York: Pocket Books, 1975], n.p.)

Probably most of us have our moments of being like Neil. If these moments take us, like Neil, straight to God to ask him the question, then that's great. My parents were devout Buddhists, and I grew up knowing there was a supreme being. When I learned about Jesus and Heavenly Father, this greater faith and more perfect knowledge built on the foundation that my parents had established for me. I have never stopped being grateful for that strong foundation and for the greater knowledge that the gospel brought to me.

Faith in Christ is not a possession like a book or a lamp. It's a growing thing, like a plant, and we can build our faith in Christ until it is unshakable and unconquerable. Let me give you an example from the experience of a Frenchman named Jacques Lusseyran, who was blinded at age eight in a schoolyard accident. Even after surgery he still had absolutely no vision and no possibility of ever seeing with his eyes again. For a month or so he bumped into objects and struggled to remember, and then one day in a garden in a small town in France, he experienced a new way of seeing.

He realized that

> in him there was a light, and that light was also in all of creation. He could see the light in trees, in people, in the ocean. . . .
>
> Some time after he claimed this light, he began to wonder if it was just his imagination, so he closed his eyes as a physical ritual and tried *not* to see the light. He described himself as in a maelstrom—but even in that he was surrounded by light.
>
> He became so skilled at his new way of seeing that

during World War II he worked for the French Underground. The only man he interviewed about whom he had any doubts was later trusted by the underground organization. It was this man who betrayed the underground workers to the Nazis. Jacques spent four years in a concentration camp in Buchenwald.

[He testified of] the two truths of his life—that all human beings can see whether they have eyes or not because we all bear that light. Any joy we experience comes from within. . . . Each of us is endowed with light. . . . We can see with the vision of faith because deep inside us is placed God's own light. (Barbara Howard, "Faithful Discipleship," *Saints Herald,* Nov. 1991, p. 15)

Each one of us has the ability to develop faith in the Savior in the same way that Jacques Lusseyran developed his new way of seeing. The ability to believe is planted deep within us. We all have memories, deep below our consciousness, of being with Heavenly Father and Jesus in our premortal life. To the Saints of the latter days, Jesus made this wonderful promise: "Verily, thus saith the Lord: It shall come to pass that every soul who forsaketh his sins and cometh unto me, and calleth on my name, and obeyeth my voice, and keepeth my commandments, shall see my face and know that I am; and that I am the true light that lighteth every man [and woman] that cometh into the world." (D&C 93:1–2.)

HAVE FAITH IN YOURSELF

There are four stones in our shepherd's bag so far, four stones that you have chosen with your best attention and with the best intentions so that they will be the best and you can have the best. They include getting the best education you can, choosing the best mentors and models you can, being patient, and having faith in the Savior. Now my suggestion for the fifth stone is to have faith in yourself. And I've saved it until last because it's a special favorite of mine.

Recently I came across a humorous saying on the topic of having faith in yourself. It was set up like the sign that a bank teller props up to say "Next window, please." This sign read: "I am lost. I have gone out to find myself. If I return before I get back, please ask me to wait." I laughed when I read it, because identity isn't something we can find by putting the rest of ourselves on hold. We find out what kind of a worker we are in the very process of working. We find out how well we love other people when we're actually engaged in loving them. We find out the quality of our faith in the process of exercising faith.

Have confidence in yourself. The other four stones are nothing without this one. And you *can* have confidence in yourself as a result of what the other four stones represent: your education gives you skills to use; your mentors have shown you what kind of person to be; you have gained self-discipline through patience and persistence; and your faith in the Savior is an unshakable foundation. You have taken upon you the name of Jesus. You are a Christian, and that is a position of immense power and equally immense responsibility.

This point was forcefully made by Kay Rizzo, an author who was exploring an illegal dump where people had thrown away old bed springs and tin cans. Under the debris, she saw a battered little teapot, covered with mud. She thought it was aluminum, at best, and took it home only because she had "a conscience perpetually time-warped between the great depression and the age of programmed obsolescence." She left it on a garage shelf for weeks until she needed something to put some apple blossoms in. So she brought the teapot inside and attacked it with steel wool and scouring powder. It was grimy with sludge, layered with "tarnish and corrosion." Then she turned it over and started working on the base.

> As I scrubbed, I noticed an engraved design emerging. One by one, letters appeared beneath the persistence of my steel wool: Revere—Sterling Silver.
>
> Horrified, I dropped the teapot into the sink.

Here was an antique teapot in sterling silver that she had been gouging away at with steel wool! Well, naturally, she took it to an antiques dealer, who confirmed that it had been created two hundred years earlier by the Revolutionary War hero and silversmith, Paul Revere. He appraised it at a fabulous sum. Then she took it to an expert who restored the silver gently, and then she carried it home to an honored place—and not as a vase for apple blossoms either. But this is the point she was making about her experience:

> I saw a reflection of myself in that silver teapot. Regardless of my age or the extent of sin's corrosion, I bear the Saviour's signature.
>
> . . . That signature means . . . a royal heritage. It means I have infinite worth. (Kay Rizzo, "Buried Treasure," *Signs of the Times*, Sept. 1992, p. 30)

My dear young brothers and sisters, you do too. I suspect that your parents and teachers have often told you, "Remember who you are." That's very good advice, but I also want you to remember *whose* you are. As the apostle Paul told the Corinthians, "Ye are bought with a price: therefore glorify

God in your body, and in your spirit, which are God's." (1 Corinthians 6:20.)

CONCLUSION

We've talked about some important weapons in the fight against the giants in your life. First, try to get the very best education you can; second, choose the best mentors and models that you can; third, be patient as you work toward your goal; fourth, have faith in Christ; and fifth, have faith in yourself. Remember who you are, and remember whose you are. David remembered who he was—a shepherd boy. But he also remembered whose he was: he was a shepherd boy into whose hands the Lord had delivered the lion and the bear, and thus he could confidently state that the Lord would also deliver the giant Goliath to him. There's a powerful message in Deuteronomy for all of us, as we remember who and whose we are:

> For thou art an holy people unto the Lord thy God: the Lord thy God hath chosen thee to be a special people unto himself, above all people that are upon the face of the earth.
>
> The Lord did not set his love upon you, nor choose you, because ye were more in number than any people; for ye were the fewest of all people:
>
> But because the Lord loved you, and because he would keep the oath which he had sworn unto your fathers, hath the Lord brought you out with a mighty hand, and redeemed you out of the house of the bondmen, from the hand of Pharaoh king of Egypt.
>
> Know therefore that the Lord thy God, he is God, the faithful God, which keepeth covenant and mercy with them that love him and keep his commandments to a thousand generations. (Deuteronomy 7:6–9)

The Lord loves you. He has brought you out of your wildernesses with a mighty hand. He is faithful. He invites you to make covenants with him, and he keeps covenants with you. May you, like David the shepherd boy, be the beloved of the Lord and have your heart fixed always in faith upon the living God.

Sources

The chapters in this volume were adapted from materials originally delivered as addresses, as follows:

Chapter 1, "Strength from the Savior": Relief Society general meeting, 25 September 1993

Chapter 2, "Sisterhood and Service": Hobblecreek Utah Region women's conference, 30 January 1993

Chapter 3, "The Way, the Truth, and the Life": presented under the title "'I Am the Way, the Truth, and the Life': A Christ-Centered Life" at the Washington D.C. and the Washington D.C. East Stake women's conferences, 6 March 1993

Chapter 4, "Beyond Juggling: The Christian Life": Honolulu Stake Relief Society leadership meeting, 15 July 1993

Chapter 5, "Keeping a Balance": Monument Park [Salt Lake City] Stake women's conference, 17 April 1993

Chapter 6, "Following Him": Lehi, Utah, tri-stake women's conference, 16 January 1993

Chapter 7, "The Way of the Christian": presented under the title, "'Follow Me': The Way of the Christian," at the San Fernando California Region women's conference, 19–21

March 1993, San Fernando, California. That weekend was the first anniversary of the death of Edward Y. Okazaki.

Chapter 8, "For Such a Time As This: Faith in the Savior": presented under the title "'For Such a Time As This': Strengthening Our Testimonies of the Savior" at the Las Vegas Nevada Region women's conference, 13 March 1993

Chapter 9, "And Be Perfected in Him": Potomac Washington D.C. Region women's conference, 6 March 1993

Chapter 10, "Steadfast in Christ": presented under the title "Women Steadfast in Christ" at the Cardston-Lethbridge Alberta Canada Region women's conference, 15 May 1993

Chapter 11, "Rain and Rainbows": Seattle-Kent Washington Region women's conference, 4–5 December 1992

Chapter 12, "Therefore, Choose Happiness": Houston Texas Region women's conference, 1 May 1993, and New York Region fireside for Young Adults and Laurels, 30 October 1993

Chapter 13, "The Lord of Little Things": Portland, Oregon, women's meeting, 22 May 1993

Chapter 14, "Banzai to Bonsai: Some Thoughts for Young People": Murray, Utah, seminary, 21 January 1993

Chapter 15, "Seek Ye the Best": Women's Week Fireside, Ricks College, 28 March 1993

Index